ROUTLEDC

]

MW01119709

EMOTION AND DELINQUENCY

EMOTION AND DELINQUENCY
A Clinical Study of Five Hundred Criminals in the Making

L. GRIMBERG

Volume 177

Routledge
Taylor & Francis Group

LONDON AND NEW YORK

First published in 1928

This edition first published in 2012
by Routledge
2 Park Square, Milton Park, Abingdon, Oxfordshire OX14 4RN

Simultaneously published in the USA and Canada
by Routledge
711 Third Avenue, New York, NY 10017

First issued in paperback 2014

Routledge is an imprint of the Taylor & Francis Group, an informa business

© 1928 Kegan Paul, Trench, Trubner & Co. Ltd.

British Library Cataloguing in Publication Data
A catalogue record for this book is available from the British Library

ISBN 13: 978-0-415-50089-0 (Volume 177)
ISBN 13: 978-1-138-00821-2 (pbk)

Publisher's Note
The publisher has gone to great lengths to ensure the quality of this reprint but
points out that some imperfections in the original copies may be apparent.

Disclaimer
The publisher has made every effort to trace copyright holders and would
welcome correspondence from those they have been unable to trace.

EMOTION AND DELINQUENCY

A Clinical Study of Five Hundred Criminals in the Making

By

L. GRIMBERG

M.D.

LONDON

KEGAN PAUL, TRENCH, TRUBNER & Co. Ltd.

BROADWAY HOUSE : 68-74 CARTER LANE, E.C.

1928

MADE AND PRINTED IN GREAT BRITAIN BY
M. F. ROBINSON & CO., LTD., AT THE LIBRARY PRESS, LOWESTOFT.

TABLE OF CONTENTS

		PAGE
	PREFACE - - - -	vii
	INTRODUCTION - - -	I
I :	HEREDITY - - - -	II
II :	PRE-PUBERTY PERIOD : THE PROCESS OF CONFLICT AND ADJUSTMENT -	36
III :	THE MAKE-UP : THE CONCEPT OF CON-STITUTIONAL INFERIORITY - -	65
IV :	MOTIVES OF DELINQUENCY - -	80
V :	ORGANIC INFERIORITY - - -	102
VI :	EMOTIONS *vs.* INTELLIGENCE - -	114
	CONCLUSIONS - - -	139

PREFACE

This book is an attempt to discuss the delinquent from the standpoint of the medical man. The subject, of course, in addition to its clinical side, has also a theoretical one, and the discussion of theories could not be avoided when it helped to elucidate some clinical aspect of the problem. The author, in the course of a number of years as a practising neuropsychiatrist, has found it impossible to look at the problem otherwise than as a physician. Primarily, the delinquent was brought to him as a medical case and as a neuropsychiatrical problem, and what was requested of him by the agency referring the *patient*, was a medical opinion. It is in this way that the author became interested in the subject.

As a neuropsychiatrist, he was, however, primarily interested in the simple questions that are put to him, daily : Is the delinquent suffering from a mental *disease* ? Are we dealing with a border-line condition, similar to a psychoneurosis ? Can mental defectiveness, so frequently found in delinquents, be held as cause for the delinquency ?

To answer these questions it meant that we had to treat the delinquent (when brought for an examination) in the same manner as any other medical case, and it was thus that the author undertook to handle the problem.[1]

The book can be rightly called a " clinical study of the delinquent ". It follows the same formulas as in

[1] The material for the book comes from the New York Neurological Institute. I wish to thank Dr. Walter Timme for the permission to make use of it.

clinical work. The first point investigated was the etiology of delinquency, and it was thus that the subject of heredity was discussed. We may call that part of the subject the remote etiological factors, whereas environment could be called the immediate. The family history would probably also enter under the same group.

The second point was the previous history of the delinquent, and the author was very careful to accept only such facts which were not under a shadow of suspicion as to their truthfulness.

The most important part of the subject was, of course, the present history and the findings on examination. It was necessary, here, to bisect every single phase of the life of the delinquent, to find, if possible, the psychopathological manifestations (if any), and at the same time to keep in mind the relationship between those psychopathological states and the accepted normal.

It is the nature of the work, itself, which prohibited the display of an array of statistics. Though the author is acquainted with the old and the modern works on the subject, he felt that the angle from which he treated the subject did not permit statistical discussions. He was not interested in delinquency as a social manifestation ; he was, here, not interested in the various theories and problems from the standpoint of the sociologist or criminologist ; he was interested in the delinquent as a human being, as a patient, and he was careful to maintain that relationship which does, and should always exist, between patient and physician.

Most of the recent works on the subject were done by a group only slightly allied to the physician. The psychologists, and only a certain class of the so-called psychopathologists, have of late been very active in gathering material, cataloguing cases and classifying the delinquents into various mental categories. There is no doubt that their work is excellent and beneficial, but an abnormal mind and an abnormal emotional make-up is not only a subject for a psychogalvanometric

study. Psychopathology deals with a diseased condition
of the mind, and as such it should be studied by those
who are able to grasp the difference between the normal
and abnormal.

There is another fallacy into which a great many
psychologists have fallen. In their discussion of the
dynamics of the mind, the organic factors, they came
face to face with the problem of endocrinology. The
behaviour psychologists have carried on experiments,
in the laboratory, and they have drawn conclusions,
especially on the subject of emotions, which are far
from being proven. As a matter of fact, we are only
suspecting the importance of the endocrines, and the
actions or interactions of all these glands is mostly a
question of debatable theories.

However, the author of this book is inclined to
believe that psychopathology has an organic basis.
He believes that constitutional inferiority is the result
of an organic inferiority, and he places that organic
inferiority in the defective endocrine system.

The delinquent, therefore, becomes a subject to
be analysed by the physician and to be looked upon
as any other patient·

The work, as presented here, is the result of the
combined efforts of a number of workers. The psychological tests were the work of Miss Gladys Tollman
of the New York Neurological Institute. Her advice
and help was of great benefit to the author. Mr. Jack
Negru, former Editor of the *Chemical and Metallurgical
Journal*, was very kind in giving valuable hints for the
classification of the material. The author's secretary,
Miss Ann Sherman, went over the manuscript and
made many improvements. Much credit, too, is due to
the author's wife, who patiently discussed with him every
phase of the subject and gave him many valuable
suggestions.

EMOTION AND DELINQUENCY

INTRODUCTION

I

The law of the State of New York defines a mental defective as :

> " Any person afflicted with mental defectiveness from birth or from an early age to such an extent that he is incapable of managing himself and his affairs ; who for his own welfare and the welfare of others or the welfare of the Community, requires supervision, control or care, and who is not insane or of unsound mind to such an extent as to require his commitment to an institution for the insane, as provided by the insanity law."

This definition may be satisfactory for legal purposes, and gives in a few words all that is assumed to be necessary to establish mental defectiveness ; from the medical standpoint, however, it is neither accurate nor satisfactory. It is not correct because to the medical man this definition deals only with the aments, the imbeciles and the idiots ; and it is not satisfactory because by . proper training and changes in their daily activities and surroundings many so-called mental defectives may become capable of taking care of themselves and their affairs.

According to the above legal definition, once a person is declared a mental defective, he or she requires to be placed under guardianship indefinitely.   Yet, it is a known medical fact that many so-called mental defectives can be reclaimed.

The law is, to a great extent, autocratic.   It does not provide and does not even attempt to prescribe the means of arriving at or establishing the fact of mental defectiveness.   Under the statute it is only necessary that a certain formula be followed, and thereupon the person in question is declared to be a mental defective.

Legal responsibility has apparently nothing to do with mental defectiveness, as defined by law.   A person may be incapable of managing himself and his affairs and still be able to know what is right and what is wrong. The Courts have so declared many times.   The case of a New York boy who was electrocuted about four years ago showed clearly that there are flagrant contradictions between the legal and medical definitions of mental defectiveness and legal responsibility.   That boy took part in a hold-up of a ticket agent in a Bronx subway station.   He was caught together with his companions. They were all found guilty of murder and sentenced to death.   The boy's attorney obtained the opinions of some of the ablest men in the State of New York, men who had distinguished themselves in the field of neuropsychiatry, and they all agreed that the boy was a mental defective with a very low intelligence quotient.   But according to the law, for that boy to have been a mental defective he should not have " been able to take care of himself and his affairs " ;   whereas, as a matter of fact, he worked and earned a living.   He attended Church occasionally, and he was able to say that killing a man or stealing was wrong.   It was, therefore, an established fact that the boy, although medically a mental defective bordering on imbecility, was legally responsible, and he was electrocuted.

Let us analyse the legal definition of mental defective :

" A mental defective is any person afflicted with mental defectiveness from birth or from an early age."

Of course, the law does not attempt to say what is meant by " early age ". For that matter, it may mean the first year or the first ten years of life. It surely does not mean the latter, from what I gathered in reviewing case histories. However, it is a known medical fact that a child born normally, with an apparent normal mentality, often at a later date may develop an acute infectious disease and remain mentally backward. Such a condition may arise after the first decade of life, and since the epidemic of encephalitis lethargica I have known adults showing mental retardation after an attack of illness. According to the law, these unfortunates are excluded from all the benefits that the law is meant to give them. The psychiatrist will have to look for other means of saving these people from punishment. He will have to class them among the insane.

The second part of the definition reads :

" He is incapable of managing himself or his affairs."

It is an easy task to find out whether a person is capable of managing himself. Medically, we inquire if the patient is able to dress and undress himself, to feed himself, etc. Personal cleanliness, habits, understanding, are other points. The questionnaire supplied by the Commission for Mental Defectives is sufficiently broad to lead us to draw an intelligent conclusion.

It is altogether different when we come to determine with accuracy whether a person is capable of managing his affairs. I have known defectives working and earning

a living, and, as a matter of fact, I have known defectives
raise a family. It is, therefore, a question of the kind
of affairs such people have to manage. The legal
definition, as can be seen, is, to say the least, incorrect,
and it is misleading.

II

Let us now look at the problem from the angle of
the Neuropsychiatrist.

The simplest definition of a mental defective would
be " an individual who is mentally below normal ". We
first determine the standard of a " normal ", rated at
say 100. By well-established methods of examination
we arrive at the rating of the persons examined and
class them as " normals " or as " below normals ".
We also allow a margin before a person is classified
in a certain group. For that purpose we establish the
ratio between the mental age and the chronological age,
or the " Intelligence Quotient " (I. Q.). The results
of the tests may not be mathematically correct, but
they will hardly allow us to classify a defective among
the average, or vice versa. It may call a high grade
moron a middle grade moron, but he will remain in
the moron group.

If we classify all the individuals giving an I. Q. above
.90 as average normal, all those with an I. Q. below .90
would be in the group of mentally below normal. The
defectives, therefore, have a large grouping. Grave
errors will rarely be made when dealing with large pro-
portions. Going down on the I. Q. scale, we meet groups
of mental defectives until we reach the I. Q. .30, individuals
who are ipso-facto legally irresponsible. And yet, all

the individuals with the I. Q. between .90 and .30 are without any doubt mental defectives and may remain so for the rest of their lives ; and, what is of greater importance, these individuals are the ones constituting the great problem for the community ; they are the most numerous and frequently in conflict with the law. The morons and the borderlines are far more troublesome to the welfare of the community than the relatively small proportion of the imbeciles and idiots.

From my own experience I mention the following facts : Out of forty-two delinquent minors examined during the last six months, I have found only twelve giving an average I. Q. All the others were mentally below normal. The twelve giving the average quotient were accused of waywardness and incorrigibility. Those giving a quotient placing them among the borderlines were arrested as incorrigibles and for petty larceny and prostitution. But those showing distinct mental defectiveness were arrested for serious offences.

The various prison surveys and the reports of the special prisons in the State of New York show the number of defectives among the convicts. Lately a special prison was established for minor delinquents classed as defectives. But it is after all a prison, the object being punishment as a deterrent or for the purpose of reformation. These special prisons were established after the endeavours of a group of people had forced the hands of the State, and they are functioning by the goodwill of the present régime. It will exist as long as the régime is in harmony with the idea, but it has no legal force behind it, for the law is conclusive in its definition of mental defectiveness. Moreover, it may transfer into the special prison delinquents accused of any crime, beginning with larceny and ending with murder.

III

From what has been stated above, it follows clearly that there is no harmony between the present legal definition and the legal opinions. I may also add here that the law has disregarded something which is of greater importance in dealing with the problem, namely, the rôle played by emotions, the emotionality of the defectives.

It is unfortunate that we have no means, as yet, of measuring emotionality. We are able to measure the mentality of an individual and classify him more or less correctly, but we are unable to measure his emotionality. I believe that the emotionality of a delinquent is far more important than the mental status. I have studied many mental defectives with this in mind, and I have found that among defectives there are some who will never become delinquents and others who will; I have found defectives who take life seriously, talk and act like grown-ups, and are anxious to imitate the ways of respectable citizens; and I have also seen defectives who were devoid of the possibility of understanding the difference between right and wrong, were childish in their behaviour and outbursts, and enjoyed acting like children, and yet were not delinquents. On the other hand, I saw others who were mentally in the same groupings, and they were always in the clutches of the law. However, in studying the emotionality of these defectives, I found that a defective classed, for example, among the morons may show the emotionality of a normal individual, in the same way that a normal individual may show emotional defectiveness.

It was, therefore, not peculiar that I found among delinquents with a normal mental status, emotional defectiveness. If the mentality had been the deciding factor in their lives, they would never have been delinquents; but it was not the mental status, not their intelligence, but the way they reacted to certain stimuli, their emotional status, which decided their delinquency.

Even among quite normal individuals, those who never come in conflict with the law, we discover different emotional reactions. We are in the habit of classifying people in that respect as sanguine individuals, or temperate individuals. Popularly, we call some people cool, and others warm. As a matter of fact, it is the emotionality of the individual that we are classifying, and when face to face with certain acts they have committed, we say that it was their sanguine temperament or cool temperament which determined the committing of the act. And in all these normal individuals a normal intelligence was present, to sway at the critical moment the committing of the acts, and a long training in the process of emotional adjustment helped make the intellect the master over the emotions.

The low average person, the moron and the mental defective in general, can be distinguished from the normal person by the fact that, in the former, the intellect to control the emotions is lacking. Emotions have no cognitive elements. The impulse of the moment is dominant and takes full control. The primitive animal instinct of self-preservation is the only impulse to action. The aim is pleasure and the avoidance of pain. If no other circumstances intervene sufficiently strong to sway the emotions, the act will be committed. I found that most of the delinquents never laid plans, never formulated a plan of what they were going to do. Some of the mental defectives are gentle, quiet, giving an appearance of intelligence. They cry easily and lie easily. They pass from tears to laughter, they smile and are sad ; they are ready to admit and agree with one, and very often to obey and do what they are told. They are what we call unstable, emotionally so. Their emotions are primitive, they have the simple emotions of childhood, but those emotions easily pass into passions and become overwhelming, destructive. They very rarely become delinquents on their own initiative ; they are mostly tools of others, and they never assume a leading rôle.

IV

More importance ought to be attached to the emotional aspect than to the question of the mentality. It is not sufficient to determine the I. Q. and classify the delinquent accordingly. It is true that the means at our disposal for the determination of emotional stability are as yet crude, but they have given definite and satisfactory results. There is really no reason why the law should not require the use of all the scientific methods available to determine the status of an individual, when that individual comes under the jurisdiction of the law for a criminal offence. In cases of insanity, since the reform movement started, under the influence of the Lombrosian school, the law has used all the means possible for determining the sanity of an accused. And yet, the number of the defective delinquents is far greater than that of the insane. The law in this respect has not listened to the voice of medicine, and even to-day prosecuting attorneys will ridicule the findings of scientific medicine.

I allude, here, to the investigation of the endocrine system.

The Great War has taught us many lessons, and among them it has taught us to value the importance of the endocrine system in matters of emotionality. This was an important field for the neuropsychiatrist, who, by his investigation, was able to determine the probable emotional disturbances of future soldiers. A soldier showing a disturbance of the thyroid, for example, was unquestionably a potential nervous wreck; a poor risk for the front, a future patient of the psychiatric department. Soldiers thus afflicted were doing better work behind the lines. It was a process of weeding out the fit from the unfit. Studies of this kind carried on after the war showed that the endocrines played a significant rôle in the emotionality of a defective, and that their dysfunctioning was the probable cause of emotional instability.

The endocrine defect in a mental defective can be conceived as a true organic inferiority, to which corresponds a psychic inferiority. In the numerous mental defectives that I have examined, I have rarely failed to find endocrine defects—as a rule a pluriglandular condition, with one gland or another predominating. The degree of endocrine defect does not go hand-in-hand with the degree of mental defect, so that a decidedly mental defective may show less endocrine disturbance than a slightly defective individual. It is in that way that we are able to explain why some defectives are delinquents and others are not, and why some normal individuals show emotional instability, whereas others are emotionally normal.

The driving force of our actions is not the intellect. In reality, the intellect is the controlling power. The driving forces are our emotions, and their stability is determined by the condition of our endocrine system.

It was with such thoughts in mind that I approached the problem, when I studied the number of delinquents who came under my observation. This view took a far clearer shape as I examined delinquent after delinquent, and finally I came to definite conclusions which form the substance of the pages to follow.

I

HEREDITY

" A child between the ages of six months and two years can be moulded into a criminal or a respectable citizen. There is no heredity ! " Thus a leader in modern psychology expressed himself a short time ago at a meeting of the N. Y. Neurological Society, and to emphasize his disbelief in heredity he added : " If fertilization of two human cells could be accomplished in vitro, then heredity would be proven false."

The behaviour psychologists take one very important sociological factor—environment—and attempt to raise to the position of a " force créatrice." By way of disproof, however, the story of Mary F. is interesting.

Mary F. was a young girl of sixteen, with an investigated life history. At the age of three months she was abandoned by her mother. At the age of four months her mother appeared to claim her, and was promptly arrested. The mother was a woman of bad reputation, living in concubinage with a labourer of similar character. She abandoned Mary F. on account of a quarrel with her " man ", who denied paternity. The child was not returned to the mother, but for her first year of life lived in an institution, until her foster-parents adopted her. She was cared for properly, and as she was a clever child—precocious in many ways— she was well liked ; and so Mary F. grew up, passed out of the public school at the age of thirteen, and entered high school. Mary F. did not know of foster-parents. To her they were her parents, and she unquestionably grew up with the same feelings of love and respect that an ordinary child has. And yet, her mother (foster) was called to school when Mary was in her second term of high school, and the principal and the teacher had many things to say. " Mary was an intelligent girl, but stubborn, egotistic and, above all, quarrelsome, destructive and immoral." Mary F. cried that evening when her mother reproached her for her bad behaviour, and promised to reform, but her mother was more attentive and careful, from then on. Small trinkets were occasionally missing from the house, little money would disappear, and her mother suspected her. At the age of fifteen Mary F. disappeared, and was gone for one night, returning with a story of two bad men who kidnapped her in an automobile. The story was pure fancy, as Mary herself admitted to a detective investigating the case. However, she kept going to school, but when she was sixteen her mother was dumbfounded to receive a note stating that Mary F. was away for the entire term. She then disappeared. She was arrested, one week later, during a raid on a " speak-easy ", and as her parents refused to have her back, she was sent to a reformatory.

This is the story of Mary F., but seventy-nine other girls show a similar life history. These seventy-nine girls were brought up in institutions or by strangers from their early childhood on. Their parents were unknown to them. Thirty-six had the advantage of being taken from their parents before the age of one year, and at no subsequent date were their parents or their family history revealed to them. From early childhood on, they were brought up in an atmosphere

of religious reverence, discipline and altruism, and yet,
with the onset of puberty they showed a reversal to
parental psychic make-up, and a short time later to
delinquency.

I am sure that the story of Mary F. and of the other
seventy-nine girls is a common occurrence to every
student of the problem, and every neuropsychiatrist
can bring proof that environment, though very important,
does not disprove heredity.

In the strict biological sense, heredity means that
the children inherit the physical characteristics of their
parents. It is the peculiarity of all organisms to transmit
their own shape upon their descendants. From the
egg of an eagle appears an eagle of the same shape, and
not only the general typus is transmitted, not only
the character of the species, but the individual peculiari-
ties of the children resemble those of their parents, both
in men and also in the lower animals. In the lower
organisms, like the simple protoplasmatic cell organism,
heredity is nothing else but a continuation of growth,
or as Weismann puts it[1], " a continuation of the individual whose living substance increases by assimilation ". As a matter of fact that is exactly what takes
place. It is not a new individual organism which is
born, but the same organism, after reaching a certain
size, divides itself. The unicellular organism divides
into two parts, the parts resemble each other, and each
part is a direct continuation of the first.

The example given above is the simplest way in
which heredity can express itself. If there is in such
an organism a psychic individuality, the parts resulting
from the division of the antecedent cell would contain
the individuality of the first. We would have not only

[1] Weismann, A.: *Das Keimplasma*. [E.T. *The Germ Plasm* (1893).]

a continuation of growth as far as the protoplasmatic body is concerned, but also a continuation of the psychic individuality.

Not so simple are matters with the organisms which multiply themselves sexually. In the first place, to obtain a descendant, it is necessary to have two organisms. We have two different cells which enter into co-operation, which coalesce, to a certain degree, and the result is one organism. During the early part of the discussion on heredity, the great concern of the embryologists was to discover how it is possible that from the coalescence of two cells, unicellular organisms, there should ensue a multicellular organism. Of course, the theories put forward were numerous, and from all these theories the one of Darwin [1] had the merit of being advanced with the intention of explaining the acquired characters. At any event, all those theories are at present chiefly of historical importance, and the theory of Weismann himself is now somewhat out of place. He explained the question by the fact that a division of physiological work determines that certain cells form into germinative cells. According to Weismann, there are in the molecular structure of the germinative cell all the conditions present which will determine the variation of the resultant individual. " It is a reversal of the true point of view to regard inheritance as taking place from the body of the parent to that of the child. The child inherits from the parent germ cell, not from the parent body, and the germ cell owes its characteristics not to the body which bears it, but to its descent from a pre-existing germ cell of the same kind. Thus the body is as it were an off-shoot from the germ cell. As far as inheritance

---

[1] Darwin, C. : *The Origin of Species.*

is concerned, the body is merely the carrier of the germ-
cells which are held in trust for coming generations."[1]
In discussing the theory of Weismann, R. H. Lock gives
a very good explanation in the following passage :
" If we consider the cells which build up an adult organ,
and for the moment regard each separate cell as an
individual, we see that each of these individuals possesses
an ancestry of cells stretching right back to the fertilized
ovum—the single cell in which the organism originated.
So far as the later cell divisions are concerned, the cell
lineage of a particular organ is separate and distinct
from that of the cells from any other organ. At a certain
distance back in the history of the organism, we shall
come across a common cell-ancestor for the cells belonging to a pair of neighbouring organs, and the more widely
separate the parts to which the cells we are considering
belong, the further back we must go before we find their
ancestry merging in a single cell. In a similar way as
with other organs, so it is found that the sexual cells
or germ-cells of an adult organism have a history quite
distinct from that of the cells from any other part of
the body, and these cells are the only ones which are
concerned in the formation of the offspring. Thus
we see that the particular cell-lineage leading up to the
germ-cells is the only one which is continued into another
generation ; all the others terminate with the death
of the individual creature of which they form a part.
From this point of view, we may consider the nature
of a given series of animals as being determined only
by the particular series of cells which constitute the
direct ancestry of the germ-cells in each individual."[2]
It is, therefore, practically a continuity present, and the
important element is the germ-cell.

[1] Wilson : *Cell Development and Inheritance*, p. 13.
[2] Lock, R. H. : *Variation, Heredity and Evolution*, 1910, pp. 73, 74.

The biologists showed a great interest in the study of the subject. The divergent opinions refer to the part of the germ-cell which is the actual carrier of heredity. The process of the coalescence of the two cells called by Weismann "amphymixis" did not explain that, but the work of Oskar Hertwig and others[1] attached the only importance to the chromatin. Weismann assumed that a change in the molecular structure of the germ-cell will determine the appearance of changes in the offspring, a thought which, though theoretical, has a great deal of plausibility. It is still the original germ-cell, as Lock puts it, but the structural changes determine variants, back-strokes, etc. Life, environment, impressions during life, determine the changes in the germ-cell, and those changes show the variants in the descendants.

In neuropsychiatrical investigations a great deal of confusion exists, at times, in reference to heredity. We erroneously speak of heredity when from alcoholic parents are born children who are mental defectives. There is no doubt that a lesion of the germ-cell of the parent may determine a defect in the offspring, but what we really have in such cases is the transmission of a defect (inborn anomalies), and no heredity. Only when no exogenous factors come into play, when no outside influences (like alcohol, syphilis, etc.) have made their impression upon the germ-cells, are we able to speak of heredity.[2]

[1] Hertwig, O.: *Allgemeine Biologie*, Jena. See also Forel's theory regarding blastophory. It is erroneous to attribute to one individual the explanation of the facts. From Galton down to Hertwig we find that there was a gradual development of the theory. As a matter of fact, Francis Galton in his *A Theory of Heredity* pointed the way for future clarification.

[2] Hoffman, Hermann: *Ergebnisse der psychiatrischen Erblichkeitsforschung endogener Psychosen*, in *Zeitschrift für die gesamte Neurologie und Psychiatrie, Referate und Ergebnisse*, Vol. 17, 1919, pp. 192-273.

However, a disease or a diseased condition is never transmitted. What is really transmitted by heredity is a predisposition to a disease, though we are entirely unable to understand the factors at play, and the nature of the biological process.[1]

This sharp demarcation between heredity and transmission of inborn anomalies appears more striking when the investigation refers to delinquents. Broadly speaking, we class all the factors which determined changes in the germ-plasma of the parent or parents, and which were responsible for anomaly in the offspring, as hereditary factors. We put in this group alcohol, lues, possibly lead, tuberculosis, rheumatism, etc. A number of authors—following the methods of the eugenic school— have compiled genealogical tables of delinquents. Yet all that those tables show is a progressive degeneracy from parent to child, with the various factors, mostly alcoholism, playing havoc in this process. All through the works of the writers we are impressed by the great confusion which exists on the subject, and even Cyril Burt, in his excellent book, speaks of heredity and of inborn anomalies as of one and the same thing.[2]

These factors are only of etiological importance. They are contributory towards the birth of congenitally defective individuals. They determine inborn anomalies, and unquestionably aid towards the appearance of degenerated generations with subsequent sterility.

Many workers have shown experimentally the importance of these factors. Stockard and Papanicolaou, in experiments covering a period of five years, have

[1] I will not enter here into a discussion of the subject of heredity. Those interested in the subject from the medical standpoint should not fail to consult the work of Francis Galton : *Hereditary Genius*, London, 1892.

[2] Burt, Cyril : *The Young Delinquent*, London and New York, 1925. Chapter on Hereditary Conditions.

shown the influence of alcohol in various generations of guinea pigs.[1]   The effect upon the parental germ-cell was so great that all the offspring deviated from the normal.   The third generation was unable to reproduce, and all showed evidence of grave deformities and other abnormalities.   This was distinct evidence of degeneracy.

In human beings, experiments of this kind are, of course, impossible.   We possess, on the other hand, sufficient statistical data to enable us to judge this progressive degenerative process.   The Swiss writer, Demme, studied twenty families with that in mind.[2] Ten of the families were not addicted to alcohol, and ten were drinkers.   In the first ten families he had counted sixty-one descendants, and in the second ten families fifty-seven descendants.

Normal families :

    a—50 children were normal
    b—7 died during the first week after birth
    c—2 were mental defectives
    d—2 showed deformities

The families where alcohol was an addiction :

    a—10 were normal, two of whom became alcoholics
    b—25 children died during first week after birth
    c—12 were idiots
    d—5 hydrocephalics
    e—5 epileptics

Similar results were obtained by Legrain,[3] who investigated fifty-four adults, survivors of fifty families, where

[1] Stockard, C. and Papanicolaou, G.: *A Further Analysis of the Hereditary Transmission of Degeneracy and Deformities by the Descendants of Alcoholized Mammals*. American Naturalist, February, 1916.

[2] Combe, A.: *Névrosité de L'enfant*, pp. 86, 87.

[3] Aschaffenburg : *Das Verbrechen und Seine Bekämpfung*, 1903, p. 56.

both parents were addicted to alcohol. He found that
sixty-five per cent. of the descendants were alcoholics
themselves, and forty-four per cent. were insane.

The work of the authors quoted above is eclipsed
entirely by the careful and scientific work done by
Prinzing. He based his conclusions upon official records
of prisoners in Germany and took into consideration
the scientific methodology of statistics. It is not only
a matter of collecting data, but of careful scientific
method in assessing the data.[1]

Prinzing studied the statistical material in Germany
during the period of 1880 up to 1888, and divided it into
two groups. In Prussia during the period of 1880-1886,
there were confined in the insane asylums a total of
52,574 insane. By a careful analysis of these cases he
was able to prove the transmission of a congenital psychic
defect (he calls it heredity) in 13,017 patients. Moreover, he found alcohol addiction in parents in 1,725
patients. During the second period, 1886-1888, there
was a total of 32,068 patients showing the transmission
of a congenital psychic defect, and in 7,762 patients
alcohol could be held responsible for the insanity.[2]

From the few figures quoted above (and innumerable
instances could be given), it is clearly seen that real
heredity in the scientific sense does not occur as
often as is suspected, but that transmutation and transmission of psychic defects is very frequent. We see the
appearance of degenerative moral and mental states in
the descendants of alcoholic parents ; but it is my
opinion, in studying carefully a few selected cases, that
the parents did show, in addition to alcoholism, a distinct

[1] Prinzing : *Trunksucht und Selbstmord*, p. 76.

[2] Kraepelin found, in his study of 1313 patients (insane) admitted
in 1905 to his clinic, 45 per cent. showing alcohol as the cause of the
insanity. (Quoted by W. Schallmayer : *Vererbung und Auslese*, p. 484.)

neuropathic state, and were below par mentally and morally.[1]

In the majority of cases, alcoholism affects one parent only, and usually the father. But in mating, or in the production of offspring, we are dealing with the coalescence of cells from two individuals of the

___

[1] Case : R. Girl servant, factory hand, seventeen years old, born in America of foreign born parents.

Family : Her mother died six years ago. She was working and kept up the home. Her father is a baker, but rarely does any work. He is addicted to alcohol and leads an immoral life. He is rarely at home, is very brutal, and does not care what happens to the children. However, he supports them, but not in a satisfactory manner. He is an ignorant man of very bad reputation, often in conflict with the law.

Past : Very little definite information could be obtained about the girl's childhood, but apparently it was the normal one of a child of the tenements, with an immoral father. After her mother's death, the girl assumed the duties of a mother by keeping house and bringing up the young child that was left. She also had to cook for her father and herself. During the day she went to school. She never graduated, but left school at the age of fifteen, ostensibly to go to work, but she did very little work, as she had to keep house. It appears, from the investigation, that the girl was not of a steady character. She ran around with the boys of the neighbourhood and would stay out late at night. There was no supervision.

Four months ago she met a man whom she knew by sight. He was a taxi driver and invited her for a ride. She was ruined by him, and forced into a life of prostitution. He subsequently threatened her with death if she dared to tell anyone. She was compelled to turn over the money to him and he would bring men to her. After a quarrel with him, he threatened to kill her and she ran to the first policeman she met and asked him to protect her.

However, she gave a fictitious name of the man, and refused to divulge his home address. Her language was the typical slang of the underworld. Asked why she refused to give the name of the man, she at first stated that she was afraid that he would kill her ; that his " pals would square it ", and then she remarked that she was not " a rat ", that she does not " squeal ".

Finally, she gave a name and an address to the examiner, but upon investigation it was found that these were also false.

Examination : The physical examination was negative, except a large thyroid and slightly bulging eyes.

Mental Examination :

> Age : 17 years, 4 months, 12 days.
> Terman Score : 12 years, 1 month
> Intelligence Quotient : .75

This quotient places the girl in the border-line group. She is inclined to play to the gallery and to give voice to many lamentations concerning her condition, blaming her father for everything.

On the test, her basal age is X. In the year XII she succeeded in all the tests except the ball and field. In the XIV year she failed all tests, except the problems of fact. Her upper limit was the average adult group.

opposite sex. It is, therefore, easily understood that in some cases the descendant may show the defect, and in other cases not. Therefore, it is readily explained why in a family one child may show such a condition and another child be perfectly normal. It is a question of the ascendancy in reproduction and in transmission of taints of one parent over another. The question of atavism should be considered where the child born may possess the characteristics of ancestors generations back. The laws of heredity go back sometimes as far as eight generations, and a child can, therefore, show the characteristics of eight generations back. In general, however, it has been proved that alcoholism in particular has this influence, that aside from direct heredity, i.e. —alcoholism in children—it will transmit psychic defects more easily than any other condition. It is the most responsible factor, especially in families where the father was the addict and the child in question is masculine. Kraepelin[1] has proved that boys will inherit the defects much more quickly than girls. His figures show that boys will inherit the defects twenty per cent. easier than girls on the side of the father, and girls five per cent. easier than boys from the mother. Daughters, as a rule, inherit about equally from father and mother.[2]

Although alcoholism is such an important factor, it is, on the other hand, not the only one.[3] From the

[1] Kraepelin, E.: *Zur Entartungsfrage (Zentralblatt für Neurologie und Psychiatrie*, 1908).

[2] The probabilities are (from the medical standpoint) that alcohol affects directly the pregnant woman when consumed during pregnancy. The alcohol ingested finds its way through the placental circulation to the embryo or foetus. Just how mutations would take place, cannot be told. It is possible that we are dealing with chronic alcoholic poisoning of the embryo or foetus. From the standpoint of heredity, the theory of Forel seems very plausible, although not proved. (See Forel, A.: *The Sexual Question*, and Moll. A.: *Handbuch der Sexualwischaften*, vol. i.)

[3] There is probably no subject which has been more investigated than the one on alcoholism. Hega, A. (*Zur chinesischen deutschen*,

medical standpoint, we are here considerably at variance with the accepted attitude of the layman. There are numerous conditions of the nervous system which are important factors. I will give here a short classification of various states which, in my opinion, are responsible factors in the transmission of psychic defects in children. I am basing this upon a clinical experience of years' duration, and an investigation of this point for the past five years.

Probably the most important of all are the so-called border-line states we meet in the daily dispensary practice. Patients of this type are distinctly psychopathics, their complaints are of an indefinite vague nature. They are unable to earn a livelihood, and are a burden to their families and society at large. They complain of phobias, anxieties, loss of ambition, weakness and insomnia. They become public charges and often frequent the dispensary, accompanied by a social worker. Their illness is nursed along by philanthropic and semi-philanthropic organizations; they are sent to convalescent camps, and are relieved of every responsibility in life. These are the typically mal-adjusted individuals, unable to cope with the rush of life—not the difficulties of life; they are the so-called neurasthenics of the olden times, anxiety states of to-day, and, in plain words, failures. However, psychiatrically, they form a very interesting group of patients. They frequently show paranoid trends, they are discontented, they blame life and society at large for their failures, and show an over-developed ego. I frequently discover in them the

---

und amerikanischen Kriminalistatistik, 1914, quoted by Schallmayer, W. : *Vererbung und Auslese*) is decidedly against the influences attributed to alcohol in the production of delinquency by its possible action upon the germ-cell. However, the statistics of Prinzing, which are the most complete, give a different impression.

simple dementia precox, the schizoid individual, the slight, practically unobservable manic or manic-depressive individual, the thymic type of man or woman. Even mentally, they do not sparkle ; they are for the most dull, border-line, or even morons. Epileptoid trends, which many times are put down as hysterical spells on account of the inability of control, are often met with. It is significant that these individuals are never alcoholics and never showed alcoholism. As a matter of fact, their egotism being so marked, they are very careful about themselves and their mode of living, and appear to be of a healthy physique.

The second group which are of importance to our study are the individuals with a tendency to a peculiar form of unpunishable delinquency. These are the people who live by their wits ; people who barely escape coming into conflict with the law. These people are for the most part clever, exceptionally so, but cleverness does not mean intelligence. They cunningly conceal their true character and pass through life earning an easy living, but are victims of venereal diseases, of alcoholism and gambling. The family life of these individuals is interesting, from the point of view that the wife earns " the living ", that they have no responsibilities in bringing up the children, that their life is generally immoral, and that the home atmosphere is frequently a continuous round of quarrelling and fighting.

We have a third and very important group—the mental defectives. It is unfortunate that the mating of defectives is not prohibited by law, and that it cannot properly be supervised. In very serious matters we too often adhere to the letter of the law, and this is one crime committed in the name of the law. All our eugenic laws can easily be defeated in the name of personal liberty, and yet, probably very grave responsibility for the production of crime and delinquency in general rests with the mating of defectives. The same applies to the fourth group of our classification —the insane.[1] Just as there is no law to forbid the marriage of defectives, so there is no law to forbid the marriage of the insane. As a matter of fact, the popular belief among some of our immigrants, that cases of insanity can be cured by marriage, is often the cause of the marriage of an insane woman to an apparently healthy man. There can be no doubt about the results. I refer the reader to the remarkable work by E. Rüdin, who studied the problem especially in relation to dementia precox and various schizophrenic types.[2] In reference to this problem, the German psychiatrists have con-

[1] This subject lends itself to a variety of controversies, and it is also important from the fact that a great many men of unquestionable genius were direct descendants from the insane. However, on closer analysis of some of the records it appears that what we term insanity, in many of the antecedents of these people, was really a psychotic trend and no actual insanity. *Robert Schumann* was the son of a nervous, melancholy father and a somewhat " peculiar mother". One brother and one sister were insane. It seems certain that the father and two of the children suffered from schizophrenia. Robert Schumann himself died insane.

Tschaikowski was the grandson of an epileptic and he himself was an epileptic. *Dostoievski* was an epileptic, and a descendant of epileptics. *Beethoven* was the son of an alcoholic and his mother died of tuberculosis. *Schopenhauer*, too, was of insane ancestry. It seems that the practical application of eugenic methods — sterilization —might not be very beneficial to the world in many instances. (Cf. Jacoby, Paul : *Études sur la selection chez l'homme*, Paris, 1904 ; Lombroso, C. : *Der Verbrecher*, Leipzig ; Idem : *Entartung und Genie*, Leipzig, 1894 ; Galton, F. *Hereditary Genius ;* and Moll, A. : *Handbuch der Sexualwissenschaften*, vol. ii. chapter on Eugenik.

[2] Rüdin, Ernst : *Studien uber Vererbung und Entstehung geistiger Störungern*. 1. Zur Vererbung und Neuentstehung der Dementia, Praecox, 1916. See also Bumke, Oswald : *Über nervöse Entartung*. Antiquity offers more examples of foresight and social legislation in this respect than our contemporaneous civilization. In Sparta not only improper mating was punished (like insane or defective), but children below par *physically* or mentally were killed. The old Hebrews prohibited marriage with epileptics or *immoral* women. At present laws are in force in many parts of the U. S. for sterilization of defective or insane in *selected* cases (see Oregon law). Similar laws were enacted in Sweden.

tributed with their well-known thoroughness to the elucidation of the problem.

The numerous case histories collected in Germany showed clearly that not only are psychoses, especially the schizophrenias, transmitted, as such, to children, but, if the psychosis is not transmitted, a degenerative trend will be found. It is, in one word, the heredity of an " Anlage ", of a fundamental psychological structure, due to a defective germ-cell. Not only that, but combinations may take place, of various blends, in some psychoses. Acute forms may never appear, and in their place we may have a chronic, or what we may call a sub-acute, light, but permanent form of the disease. This class of psychotics are, on account of their paranoid trends, easily developed into criminals of the murderous type, revenging crimes on account of slight and imaginary insults or supposed injustices done them.

A somewhat similar state we find when studying epilepsy in relationship to crime. " Premeditated criminal acts by epileptics," said Spratling, " are not common, though I recall several cases in which the motive was flimsy and the degree of injury sought to be inflicted out of all proportion to the apparent sense of personal grievance the epileptic based his assault upon."[1]

It is interesting to give here some data about heredity and delinquency. Sarlo studied the inmates of two institutions, eighty-nine delinquents in each institution. He selected a reformatory and a protectory, and he found the following facts in regard to the transmission of defects which may be responsible for delinquency following neuropathic heredity :

[1] Spratling, William, P. : *Epilepsy and Its Treatment.* (Philadelphia, 1904, p. 497.)

	Reformatory	*Protectory*
Alcoholism	15	11
Psychopathic and neuropathic heredity	12	11
Criminal heredity	9	26
Tuberculosis and rickets	18	16

From these figures it can be seen that, although alcohol plays a great rôle, it does not occupy the foremost place.[1] It is unfortunate that during the time when Sarlo did his work our methods of investigating syphilis were not far advanced, or he would have added that also.

Lino Ferriani studied 2,000 juvenile delinquents and found that 701 were the children of very immoral parents, 169 of questionable character, and 53 of entirely degraded parents. However, only 207 of the 2,000 delinquents were brought up and lived together with their parents.[2] Kurella's material is probably more important, as it shows the actual relationship between the various conditions of the parents and the delinquency of the children. 1,714 delinquents showed (based on the statistics of Sichard) in parents :[3]

1. Crime   43.7 per cent.
2. Mental Disorders   6.7   ,,
3. Epilepsy   1.7   ,,
4. Alcoholism 16.2   ,,

There is a certain group of organic diseases of the cerebro-spinal system which undeniably plays a great rôle. This question has recently been the subject of investigation. In the first place, I will mention

[1] Aschaffenburg, l.c.

[2] Ferriani Lino : *Minderjährige Verbrecher*, German translation, p. 76.

[3] Aschaffenburg, l.c. p. 102

Huntington's Chorea. This disease is one of the hereditary diseases. Most of the cases studied (cases correctly diagnosed) were found to be hereditary. It is a disease with manifestations affecting not only the motor system but also the mind, and many such cases showed only one form, mental manifestations, whereas others showed both mental and organic.[1]

I had an opportunity to follow the family history of one patient and to obtain investigated notes about his ancestors as far back as the paternal great grandfather and maternal grandparents. The Mendelian law was practically exemplified in that family. About fifty per cent. of the descendants showed the disease in one form or another. It is my belief that that family will gradually disappear, without leaving any trace of offspring.[2] Entres has studied the disease from the point of view of heredity, and the description that he gives of the children of such patients is worth consideration. He discovered two kinds of personalities in the children of patients suffering from the disease. " Some are exceptionally nervous, irritable, secretive, cranky, nagging, revengeful, quarrelsome, sexually on the alert, with tendencies to excesses, and are hypersensitive ; whereas the others are healthy and strong from the nervous standpoint." The first group could be called, according to Rüdin, schizoid personalities, in spite of the fact that there is no relation to dementia precox.

It is important to note, here, that the description of the personalities of these children is practically the same as the personalities we meet in delinquents.

[1] Entres, Joseph Lothar : *Zur Klinik und Vererbung Huntingtonschen Chorea*, 1921.

[2] Grimberg, L.: Huntington's *Chorea*, *N. Y. Med. Jour.*, January 27, 1917. (From the father of the patient who suffered from insanity there ensued a total of 16 descendants. Of these 16, 8 were affected and 8 normal.)

The question of epilepsy has often been a subject of investigation, and no definite findings have been obtained. However, if epilepsy in itself is not hereditary as a disease, it is yet noticeable that the children of epileptic parents are not up to the mark. It certainly holds true, as various observers have found, that epilepsy associated with mental disease, especially the manic depressive psychosis, is liable to give rise in children to psychosis of the same type.

The havoc played by syphilis in the descendants is well known to everybody, and hardly needs to be mentioned here. We notice particularly the appearance of mental defectives of the worst type and their subsequent delinquency. One case is known to me, where the father was suffering from General Paresis and his oldest son from Congenital Lues. The latter, at the age of fourteen, came in conflict with the law for burglary. He had an average intelligence quotient, but he was emotionally unstable and never succeeded in getting out of the clutches of the law.

The mechanics of heredity are unknown, but it is only justifiable to assume that the mating of certain individuals will give a certain kind of offspring. There is no reason why the results that we obtain in breeding animals should not also be verified in human beings. From extensive researches on animals and from the observation of human beings, the deleterious defects which result from improper mating appear unquestionable.

I must agree with Rüdin, that in relation to human beings we cannot accept the proofs adduced by the botanists in their study of the Mendelian law. Also, that where artificial breeding is concerned, the results will be different from those where promiscuous and unsupervised mating is taking place. Statistical material, though of very great importance, cannot always be utilized successfully in connection with human beings, and therefore strict mathematical formulas cannot be established.

In following the literature on delinquency, the relationship between the state of the parents and the delinquency of the children is clearly seen. In most of the cases it is a question of transmutation, although many of the parents of the delinquents were delinquents themselves. However, delinquency is not a disease, and the important factor is the character and the make-up.

The material collected by various authors (Sarlo, Ferriani, Aschaffenburg, Rüdin, Prinzing, Magnan, Legrain, and others) offers a wealth of data proving the point. Researches, which were primarily undertaken for the purpose of the study of families of feeble-minded, also show, indirectly, the appearance of delinquency in such families as a direct result of transmission of a psychic defect.[1] The material in my possession, though not very extensive, has been studied partly for that purpose. The total number of delinquents examined was 498.

I

1.	Brought up by parents	419
2.	Brought up by strangers	53
3.	Brought up in an institution	26

II

1.	Both parents living	261
2.	Father only living	107
3.	Mother only living	93
4.	Both parents dead or unknown	37

Out of 461 with living parent or parents, 16 were taken by various agencies and put under the care of

---

[1] Notably among the works of importance are : Goddard, H. H. : *The Kalikak Family*; Dugdale, R. L. : *The Jukes, a Study of Crime, Pauperism and Heredity*.

strangers or in institutions, owing to the unsatisfactory home surroundings (moral) of the parents. A selected group of delinquents was studied, from the standpoint of heredity, and the results obtained were very important.

A group of 30 girl delinquents gave complete data, and out of this group, 12 showed parents without reproach, while 28 parents showed a defect themselves.

The term "without reproach" means that the parents in question were to all appearances adjusted to the social environment, that they were more or less successful, and that there were no mental diseases or delinquency. From the last group of 28, we must distinguish six girls where the parents were unknown. But by "parents unknown" we mean that the children were taken from their parents during their infancy on account of the parents' moral and social status. These children were placed in institutions or put in the care of selected people, or possibly relatives. From the data in my possession, the parents were not desirable and were in conflict with society. The following tables, constructed relative to these data, give a view of the relationship between the parents' status and the girls:

I

Both parents living	16
Both parents unknown	6
Father only, living	6
Mother only, living	2
	30

II

Brought up by parents	13
Brought up by strangers	16
Brought up in an institution	1
	30

An investigation of the parents' status gave the following results :

III

Good character	12
Father alcoholic	4
Mother alcoholic	1
Both parents alcoholic	1
Insanity in both parents	1
Father having bad morals	1
Mother having bad morals	2
Both parents having bad morals	1
No data obtained	7

Here, " bad morals " is a term generally meaning prostitution or concubinage. Of the two mothers classified under this head, one left her husband, took the child with her and went to live with another man. The other mother was abandoned by her husband who left the country for Europe, and then she took up housekeeping with another man. She also bore a bad reputation in the neighbourhood. The alcoholic parents showed a demoralized family life, poverty to the extreme, as well as immorality. Especially is that true in the families where the mothers were alcoholic. In the family where both parents were insane, the father suffered from general paresis, and the mother was committed to an institution (before the father's insanity) on account of dementia precox. The girl was distinctly feeble-minded, and was confined for years in an institution for feeble-minded children ; later on, she showed tendencies to a simple dementia precox. No other children were known in the family.

The table specifying that the children were brought up by strangers, means that the authorities took the child from the parents and placed her in the care of strangers on account of the immoral condition of the parents. In two instances, the relatives of the girl took her away from the parents so as to give her a proper bringing up. The parents were in all those instances incompetent and irresponsible, and could not be trusted with their children.

Considering the relationship of the moral status of the parents to the delinquency of the children, we find a group of twelve girls. According to their delinquency, we construct the following table :

Waywardness	7
Incorrigibility	2
Prostitution	3
	12

If we put waywardness and incorrigibility in the same class, it appears, therefore, that only three girls were accused of a more serious offence and that nine were accused of minor offences. It is also important to note here that the ages of these girls were from twenty to fifteen. The only girl of twenty was accused of prostitution and the only girl of fifteen also was accused of prostitution, but in the latter case it was a question of compulsory prostitution, and the girl in question showed, also, mental abnormalities with psychopathic trends. She was a schoolgirl, and left home on account of a family disagreement and fell into the clutches of a man who forced her into prostitution.

However, in these cases, there were a number of other factors at play which determined the delinquency, as will be shown later. The hereditary factor cannot be found here at first glance, but inquiries showed that the fathers of at least four cases were of a nervous temperament, that in another case the mother was of a quarrelsome disposition, and that in still another case, the mother was arrested for disorderly conduct, after a fight with the neighbours. A neuropathic trend in the parents could be found in practically all the cases, and in one case the transmission of a defect could be seen by the fact that all the children had some defect ; one sister was accused of petty larceny, another sister was a prostitute, and a brother was arrested and served a jail sentence for assault. However, the parents, as far as the law was concerned, could present themselves with a clean slate ; as far as the surroundings were concerned they were in adjustment, and were not public charges. Poverty, with the exception of one case, did not enter into play, and the family life was not demoralized.

Entirely different are the facts with the second group, where the parents were morally and socially below par. Here we find distinct defects in the parents. Alcoholism left deep furrows in the psychic make-up of the children. They were arrested for petty larceny, for immorality or for shoplifting. The early life of these children was bad, their school life was a continuous struggle with the teacher and their environment. They were mentally below par, they never graduated, they were truants and some of them came before the Children's Court. Whereas, in the first group of twelve girls, the vaginal examination showed only four who had had sexual relations, the remainder of twenty-two girls belonging to the second group *showed only two who did not have sexual relations.*[1] We recognize at a glance, in examining these girls, that there is something essentially wrong with their entire constitution ; their personalities are different from the normal, and many of them have

[1] The statistics given by Ferriani (l.c.) show similar results.

D

no insight into life. Their opinions are distorted, their views infantile, their conceptions primitive. In knowing the parental histories of these girls, and then examining the girls themselves the thought strikes one immediately, that it could not have been different ; that another form of life, another kind of life, would have been a sociological impossibility. In the shaping of life, the girls whose mothers or both parents were alcoholics showed a graver disturbance than those whose parents were purely immoral. The product of these fathers and mothers is the most tragic sequel of life ; a child weak physically, mentally and morally, bearing the imprint of lack of supervision and of improper mating.

How serious the question is can be seen from the study of three cases which are included in my report. These three girls were the product of mating of an alcoholic father and mother in one case, an alcoholic mother in another, and an alcoholic father and immoral mother in the third case. These girls were taken away from their parents at an early age. One was brought up by a relative of good moral character, and the other two were brought up by strangers. However, their school life was deplorable. One of the girls was arrested for truancy, and then put in the care of another family, as it was thought she might do better in another home. She never improved, and at the age of fifteen she had her first sexual experience with a man in the neighbourhood. She soon left school, and then disappeared from home. She was arrested in the company of doubtful characters, and her life was one of immorality and vice. The other two girls were brought up by strangers ; they never knew their parents, and yet, in spite of the respectability of their homes, they had early sexual experiences, were in trouble with the teachers, never kept a job for any length of time, and finally left home in the company of a young man with a police record. Their mental examinations gave a low intelligence quotient, they were emotionally unstable, were amoral in many respects, and were, to all intents and purposes, useless members of society.

From the further study of my cases, it will be seen that what we regard as delinquents were primarily biological products of an improper mating, with the resultant transmission of a psychic defect. To a great extent, the shaping of life of these girls was pre-destined and pre-determined, following definite biological rules, for they were born devoid of the potentiality to adjust themselves to our social order.

II

PRE-PUBERTY PERIOD

The Process of Conflict and Adjustment

We assume—and we attempted to prove that assumption—that a child brings into the world not only the physical characters of his parents, but also the psychical. He "inherits" the ultimate results of centuries and centuries of modifications which have taken place, and presents himself as the "finished" product of his species. Irrespective of which part of the germplasma is the carrier of this heredity, we must assume that not only does a physical heredity occur, but also a psychical. The normal child is born with all the characteristics which will enable him to fit in with the social organization.

We cannot possibly conceive a human being otherwise than as a social unit, and, therefore, he cannot be studied otherwise. His actions and behaviour, his normality or abnormality express only the way in which he reacts to the various social stimuli. His existence as an individual depends entirely upon the "rapport" that he is able to establish with the social organization at large, and his life during the first few years is the trial of adaptation, the attempt at subjugation of the strongest element transmitted by heredity, egotism. If by environment we understand the entire social structure which surrounds an individual, then we may

36

consider the *family* as the first environmental factor with which the child comes into conflict. I conceive this moulding of the child's life by the family as a conflict, not as a simple process of influence or training.

The first reactions of a child to its surroundings are reflex acts, those acts showing themselves in acts of defence, all with the tendency to preserve life. There are no ideational elements in the first acts of child-life, no cognitive elements. These enter into play later, after the first stimuli of varied characters have acted. Cognitive elements bring with themselves (later on) elements of judgment, of thinking, of discrimination. When cognitive elements enter into play, we may safely speak of egotism in the child, but before that, we speak of the instinct of self-preservation. " In the involuntary movements of sucking, and in the disposition to put everything grasped into the mouth, may be recognized a tendency to refer everything to self as the centre ; this centre is not, however, the object of an idea. When ideas arise of that which excites pleasure or pain, the instinct of self-preservation stirs as love or abhorrence, and assumes the character of an impulse." [1]

Egotism, therefore, represents a step higher in the development of the instinct of self-preservation, when, to a certain extent, it includes actions directed towards an aim, that of bringing pleasure. In ultimate analysis, however, it fades into the inherent and transmitted instinct of self-preservation.

" In the instinct of self-preservation," says Höffding, a little further, " lies a tendency to make the individual self the centre of existence, and this tendency continues to take effect so long as no motive arises for the recog-

---

[1] Höffding, H. : *Outlines of Psychology*—Chapter VI : " Psychology of Feeling," p. 243.

nition of other centres of pleasure and pain in the world besides self." [1]

We may conceive egotism as the most conservative element transmitted by heredity. It is the most conservative, because it is biologically the oldest. This instinct is as old as the biological unit, the cell itself. The possibility of adaptation to a medium is dependent upon the possibility of moulding this instinct, that is, the possibility of either changing the individual itself so as to be able to exist in the environment or of changing the environment. We notice this biological process in the lowest organism and in all the animal series. There is always a conflict going on between the medium —the surrounding—and the organism. The instinct of self-preservation is, no doubt, the most important directing factor which makes existence possible.

This thought was very well expressed by the late Félix Le Dantec, when he said : " A living being is the result of a struggle between two factors, the substance contained in the contour of the animal on one side, and the medium on the other ". . . . " it is the struggle between heredity, the total of transportable qualities, and training, the total of successive states of the media concerned." [2]

In the lower organisms, like microbes, this struggle can be studied in laboratories, and with the aid of the microscope. We see how the medium overcomes the bacteria when it is obnoxious to their existence, or where bacteria transform the medium, by production of substances propitious for their living.

The human being is the most helpless animal at birth. His acts are reflex acts, but the instinct of self-

[1] Höffding, H. : l.c. p. 244.
[2] Le Dantec, Félix : La Lutte Universelle, p. 73. (X Edition).

preservation is entirely nullified by the physical helplessness of the being. Even the most primitive act of self-defence, the cry, is of no use to the human being, on account of the centuries and centuries of dependence upon others, which have made him unable to recognize danger, even instinctively. The biological nature of the instinct, on the other hand, appears at the time when egotism begins to show itself, during the period of cognition and ideation.

Child life, in this respect, is marked by an over-expression of egotism, of self-assertion. A thing refused brings forth outbursts of temper, anger and destructive tendencies. I place this period very early in child life, probably during the first year of life. I have failed to find the so-called lusty cry, the cry of happiness. Invariably the cry was one of self-assertion. My personal observations on the subject lead me to believe that the cry is associated with cognitive elements. When a child cries, the cry, as a rule, is stopped when the child is picked up. To see if cognitive elements are present, I made the following observation. A child of four months was invariably picked up by myself whenever I came in contact with it. After a few days, my appearance was sufficient to make the child cry if I did not pick it up. That very same child would not cry if the mother appeared, because it was not associated with the idea of being picked up. We deal, therefore, in a child with a purposeful assertion of egotism, with a decided conscious act. However, this feeling of self-assertion that a child has, is not only an expression of the egotism, the desire for pleasure that I noticed in the child, but is also associated with another feeling which came very much to the foreground in subsequent events. When, for the purpose of trying this out, the child was left for a while crying and then subsequently picked up, he invariably stopped, but at future times his crying would be more vigorous from the very beginning. The giving in to the child leads invariably to the feeling of power, which is, of course, nothing but a stronger egotism, self-assertion. In matters of child training, the experience of every observant mother has been the same ; just as yielding to the child brings with it the feeling of powerfulness, so does the not giving-in bring the feeling of powerlessness. If the first helps towards the increase of egotism, the second unquestionably tends towards its decrease. It is the second which helps the moulding of the child's personality and the subduing of his overstrong egotism, its subjugation to the demands of others.[1]

It is impossible to say at what age sympathy begins. That requires not only an appreciation of various situations in life, in daily experiences, but also a power of comparison and a well developed memory structure in the mind of the child. The appearance of sympathy as a psychic attribute in the child's life marks the beginning of adaptation to the environment. This goes hand-in-hand with the recognition of powerlessness against other people's will and demands. In ultimate analysis, even the recognition of the dependency that the child feels towards others, the helplessness in which it finds itself, is after all nothing but an expression of egotism. The child submits to the whims and demands of others, because in that way its desires are fulfilled. It is done because it brings pleasure and self-satisfaction. But in such cases we notice that egotism has assumed a

[1] Lombroso made the following remarks : " Those moral anomalies, which in adults are called ' crimes ', are very frequent manifestations in children associated with similar outbursts, especially among the children with an hereditary *anlage*. But later in life, partly under the influence of training, they entirely disappear."

somewhat different form, that of giving in, of following others.[1]

We have, therefore, two elements in conflict : In the first place, the conservative element transmitted by heredity, egotism ; and, in the second place, the revolutionary element, the social egotism. Translated into accepted phrases, we may call the social egotism, the factor which develops altruism—the social instinct—in a person.

Throughout the above discussion, I have assumed two facts. In the first place, that the child under consideration is physically and mentally normal, and in the second place, that the family is also a normal family. It is, however, important to clarify the meaning of a normal child. Though it appears that the meaning is clear, for the purpose of our discussion, it is very important to give it a definite interpretation.

By a normal child, it is understood that the child possesses the potentiality of adjustment. We are not only born with the instinct of self-preservation, which develops into egotism as soon as cognitive and ideational elements are possible, but we are born with an ego which is able to be curbed, which is amenable to moulding. We are born with the possibility of feeling and of sympathy, and we can be conscious of such feelings.[2]

---

[1] The founder of the positivist school in philosophy expressed himself thus : " The individual life was characterized by the preponderance of the personal instincts (instincts personnels) ; the domestic life, by the appearance of sympathetic instincts ; the social life, by the development of intellectual influences. Each of these three stages of existence prepares the other in their order. The result is a co-ordination of the morals ; firstly personal, then domestic, and finally social. The first is under the careful discipline of the conservation of the individual ; the second tends to subdue egotism to sympathy ; and the third, to direct the total of our actions according to the wishes of society, always having in mind the common good." (Émile Rigolage : *La Sociologie par Aug. Comte*, 1897, p. 108).

[2] " The ideal man ", concluded Spencer, " is so constituted that all his spontaneous activities are in accord with the conditions imposed by the social environment." (Th. Desdouit : *La Responsibilité Morale* p 31).

The family is a social unit, but it cannot be conceived as an isolated unit. It must be considered as an outgrowth of the entire social organization at large. It embodies the moral concept of the entire social organization, and the institutions of that social organization are understandable to such a family.

To conceive a family as an artificial construct would be just as erroneous as to conceive that at a certain time a certain number of families could willingly and intentionally give form to or change a social organization. However, in the study of social organizations we meet with families which are mal-adjusted, not in harmony with the entire structure. It is probably on account of the inassimilability of the individual members of the family, or because the family under consideration is a negativistic trend in the social evolution. Such families are known in the neighbourhood as demoralized, trouble makers, degenerates, etc. There is no question that mating of improper persons is frequently responsible for this. Eugenics has tried to determine, as far as possible, the truth of this assertion, and though the data are very meagre at present, we are, nevertheless, in a position to say that improper mating is the most important cause of mal-adjusted families. And this is the first responsible agent in the moulding of the child's personality for the work necessary in the subsequent adjustment of the child to the social organization as a whole.

It follows, therefore, that the delinquent child is, to a great extent, not only the result of heredity, but also of a mal-adjusted family which was unable to accomplish the process of equilibration between egotism and social surrounding. It is not the fear of punishment which deters the child from delinquency, but the gradual development in himself—if living in an adjusted family—of that *internal command* (commandement intérieur) which in the ultimate analysis is nothing but the reproduction in ourselves of the external authority of the social environment. That explains, to a great extent, the old statistics, like those of Ferriani, who in an analysis of 2,000 juvenile delinquents found 910 who were the children of criminals.[1]

The case of S. is representative of a great many among the delinquents investigated in my series :

Case S   Counter girl, sixteen years old, foreign born, of foreign parents.

Family :   Her father, a man of many aliases and bad character, is living in Europe. Her mother left her father eleven years ago and came to America. She left S. and a little sister with the father. Two years ago the mother sent money for her and her sister to come to the United States. Her father lives with another woman in her home country, and she was brought up by the other woman until she came here. The mother also lives here with another man, and S. found her living with that man when she came to this country.

Past :   Nothing could be learned about the girl's past, except that she led a life of carelessness. She had never worked since she came to America, and though young, she was in friendly relations with gangsters in the neighbourhood, and was very untruthful and abusive. From her mother very little could be learned, except that the moral condition of the girl was far from satisfactory and that she was a notorious character in the neighbourhood.

Present :   She ran away from home after a quarrel with her mother. She accused her mother, before the

[1] Ferriani, *l.c.* p. 76.

desk officer at the police station, of immorality and prostitution, and had even attempted, on several occasions, to beat her mother and burn her clothes. She accused the man who was living with her mother of being the father of her sister's child, and proclaimed that the entire atmosphere in the house was immoral.

On investigation it was found that the whole family status was sordid ; but the girl was arrogant and never told the truth. At no time was she corrected. Sexual life in her home was freely displayed between her sister and the man living with her mother. She never attended church, and had no religious training.

Examination : During the examination the girl was impudent and did not answer freely. It was impossible to determine the truth from what she was relating.[1]

However, if the family is the first factor which moulds the child's personality, it is, on the other hand, not the only one. It is when this child comes into contact with

[1] Mental Examination :

> Age : 16 ? 18 ?
> Terman Score : At least 9 years
> Intelligence Quotient : .56

It was extremely difficult to obtain a satisfactory estimate of the patient's mental condition. In the first place, she considered the work more or less of a joke, laughing at inopportune times and trying to have the examiner see the situation as she saw it. Secondly, whenever a question was complicated or difficult, she fell back on the plea that she did not understand. It was the examiner's impression that she understood more than she was willing to acknowledge.

The patient definitely passed all the VIII year group. In the IX year series the alternatives were substituted for sentence construction and giving rhymes. Under these conditions, she succeeded in all tests, except the date. She knew the day of the week, but had no idea of the month or the year. In the X year, she failed on the repetition of syllables, repetitions of six digits in given order, free association test, comprehensions, absurdities and vocabularies. Credit was given her for the report of the paragraph read. She read poorly, but gave nine memories. She failed in tests of the XII year. At one time during the test the girl showed that she was under emotional strain. When corrected for laughing so much, she said, " I can't help it, I am a little crazy ". She then had the appearance of being about to cry, although she soon gained control of herself.

the outside world, with interests that may conflict with its own, with the egotistic tendencies of other children that are in direct conflict with its own, that the difficult progress is being made.   This subconscious conflict goes on during the entire school life of the child, and during that entire period the process of adjustment to the entire social organization takes place.   Of course, the school of a given social organization is a direct product of that organization.   It embodies in itself the concept of the organization, and the normal child of that structure is able to grasp these concepts and live up to them. We could not, for example, imagine a school in this country which would not pay great attention to athletics, for the nation in itself is young, attracted by feats of strength, full of the desire for freedom.   We see in school life the entire psychology of the nation ; just as in the schools of nations governed by an absolute monarch a general application of rigid rules of discipline is enforced, with the same iron hand as in the government of the country.   This second agent-school is responsible for the adjustment of the child to society, is as important as the first, and frequently it will help to eradicate the mischief done by the first.[1]   Rarely, if ever, when these two agents have failed, does the third—society at large— accomplish an adjustment.[2]   The social organization

---

[1] Twenty years ago, when the question of moral responsibility was generally discussed and a great many books were written on the subject, one author expressed himself in this way : " Education is not unilateral, where the teacher works by himself and the child is passive, like a piece of wax, ready to receive the imprint.   It is a common work, and it cannot be successful unless the child co-operates with the teacher.   It is, therefore, necessary that they both have a common aim" (Desdouit, Th. : *La Responsabilité Morale*, Paris, p. 146). However, where the author missed Herbert Spencer's reasoning, was in the fact that he forgot that the child *must* possess that potentiality of adjustment.

[2] Statistics on delinquency show, invariably, the difficulty the delinquent had as a child, in school. Dr. V. V. Anderson, in his report on 300 delinquents, shows that fifty per cent. of those examined had been in court more than once. Thirty per cent. had already received

at large assumes that the individual about to enter upon
the great conflict of life, is, if not completely adjusted,
at least adjusted to the degree of assimilability. It
a sumes the absence of conflict, at least of those conflicts which may come in sharp contrast to the tendencies
of society.   It assumes that the individual possesses
moral concepts which are in harmony with those socially
accepted.   It assumes that, without teaching, the individual already possesses the knowledge of what is right
and wrong.   It assumes that all those facts were inculcated
in the individual through the long process of personal
adjustment during the great conflict in childhood and
school life.[1]

In the United States, the entire problem has, also,
a different aspect, and the discussion of that part of
the problem will perhaps help us to understand very
vital questions which trouble us to-day.   The social
organization of this country has the distinction of being
formed by a conglomerate of various nations and races,
races which differ in many respects sharply as regards
views and primordial characteristics.   It is true that
the Anglo-Saxon apparently possesses the greatest
assimilating power any nation or race has ever shown.
At the same time, it would mean overlooking the difficulty of the problem of assimilation, if it were not
considered impartially.   We find racial groups representing

---

commitment to public institutions prior to study in the clinic, and
many had served repeated sentences at delinquent institutions.
(V. V. Anderson : *The Psychiatric Clinic in the Treatment of Conduct
Disorders of Children*, 1923, p. 37).

[1] It is the assumption of the existence of a moral instinct. " If
the moral instinct is nothing else but the social instinct, it must fight
against the egotistic instinct.   The moral instinct is the collective
force assembled in an individual.   (La force collective enmagasinée
dans l'individu.)   When we wish to oppose the force of our individual
interest to this kind of social power (puissance sociale) which resides
in us, we experience a feeling of constraint " (Fouillée : *Critique
des systèmes de Morale Contemporaine*, p. 9).

a social evolution years behind that of the Anglo-Saxons. It is true that most of the individuals of those races are perfectly normal, but they are born with the potentiality of adjustment of their own social organization. As a matter of fact they have completely adjusted themselves to their own society, and their advent to this country served only to bring forth a conflict which, in many instances, is hopeless. We notice the natural defence put up by these social and racial groups. They try to create, in the midst of the racial group foreign to them, an environment similar to their own, where they can live according to their own social and moral concepts. That is the origin of the ghettos and colonies that we find in this country. They are created as a defence against an enemy ; it is a subconscious escape from a situation ; it is the struggle of racial egotism against an enemy, which, at least in this country, ends disastrously for them. This is true not with the first generation, but with the following one.

On the other hand, the child born in the midst of such a group is in a position which presents many difficulties. Not only is there the conflict between the child and the immediate family, but also with the imposed concept from the outside, with which the family itself is in conflict. The conflict in the child of such a family is doubly severe. This is unquestionably the reason why in our great cities with a large foreign population, the majority of the delinquents are of foreign extraction. This is not just a coincidence, and is not due to the fact that our foreign element is bad, but it is a natural result of a problem which unfortunately has not been solved. It is due to the fact that efforts of adjustment in these cases did not start with the advent of the foreigner to this country.

The child born in this country of a family which has not adjusted itself to this environment, has not only to contend with the same difficulties as any other child, but with other factors as well. Primarily, the family will mould the child's personality so that it will be in harmony with their concepts and views. Though born in this country, it will be a foreigner born here. When the child finally has reached an adjustment with the family life, it goes forth to school, where it comes in contact with an entirely different concept, at variance with the concepts and views of the family. A process of adjustment starts then, anew. A conflict takes place in school and another conflict at home. It is in these varied conflicts that the difficulty of the entire problem rests, and in this fact we find the explanation of the great number of delinquents showing foreign extraction. The following case is illustrative of this point :

Case L : Clerk, sixteen years old, American born, of foreign parents.

Family : Parents are living ; the father a merchant of good character. The mother keeps house, and is also of good character. One sister is a schoolgirl. The home surroundings were good, and the parents have a good name in the neighbourhood. They were always anxious to give the girl a good bringing up, and an education. The father, however, is somewhat a free thinker, imitating the Americans (?), although not an educated man. The mother follows the religious precepts, observing the dietary but otherwise is not religious. They never gave their children a religious training.

Past : Patient was the oldest child in the family, and was somewhat " spoiled." They tried to make an " American " out of her. The second child was not born until this girl was eight years old, and for that length of time she was the only child in the house. Her mother states that she was always stubborn, quarrelsome, and wanted her own way. According to the father she rarely told the truth, and, therefore, he never " put much stock in her remarks ". They had to give in to her if they wanted peace. However, she was not a bad child otherwise, and she caused them no annoyance. She began to go to school at six, did very good work in school, and caused no trouble to the teachers. She graduated from the public school and went to high school for one year. She did not like school work. She began to go out with friends, which greatly interfered with her school work, and she left school, wanting to go to work. That was only six months ago. Since then she denied her religion, became friendly with boys in the neighbourhood and also some girls, but avoided those of her own faith. However, she soon became acquainted with bus drivers in her neighbourhood, and they allowed her to ride in the bus free of charge, in order to talk to her. She remained out late at night. Her father objected, but could not prevent her from seeking the company of these men. Three months ago she was ruined by one of the drivers, and soon she discovered that she was pregnant. She then decided to leave home.

Present: She left home and went to live with a man whom she knew by sight. He told her that he was going to get a divorce from his wife. She did not know if what he told her was true He knew that she was pregnant. Her father, in the meantime, notified the police and asked for her arrest. She was then arrested as an incorrigible and was also held as a witness.

E

The story as told by the girl and that obtained from her parents showed great discrepancies. The girl, unquestionably, was not telling the truth. There was no doubt that she had had relations with other men much before the consequences brought it to notice, and she was, therefore, unable to identify, positively, the man who was the father of her child. She showed a great deal of arrogance during the examination, frequently refused to reply, and spoke disrespectfully of her parents. She was sure that her parents would take her home. She had no religious insight at all, and stated that the only way to judge a misstep was by how one felt about it, and not by religious ethics. The world is unable to understand love, and her parents are entirely unable to understand her. They are too old-fashioned. She admitted that she was lying frequently, but did that only when she had an object in view. Her greatest anxiety was not about the pain she had caused her parents, or about her own name, but only about the outcome of her own case. She realized that she was somewhat hampered in earning a living, and that if her parents refused to take her back, she would have no place to go. That worried her more than anything. She intended to shield the man with whom she was living, claiming that she had told him she was more than twenty years of age. When confronted with the fact that he knew her family, and had known her since she was a child, and that he knew she had just left school a year before, she said she had told him otherwise. She showed no remorse, answered frequently in monosyllables or did not answer at all. She thought that the greatest handicap in her life was her mother's fanaticism. She disliked her own parents; they are cruel and cannot forgive.

Examination : The general physical examination was negative.

Mental Examination : (By the psychologist) :

Age : 16 years, 3 months, 22 days.
Terman Score : 15 years, 9 months.
Intelligence Quotient : .98.

This quotient places the patient in the average group. She gives the total impression of being able to obtain a somewhat higher score if she tried. She went through the tests in a perfunctory manner, showing little interest in success or failure. At no time did she exert herself to try hard and persevere on the more difficult questions. If she considered them difficult, she gave a reply which showed that there was very little thought behind it. She was exceedingly reticent, and did not talk freely about herself. Her replies came mostly in monosyllables. Towards the latter part of the examination she showed signs of fatigue, and her attention wandered from the test to different noises in the street.

On examination, her basal age is nine years. She succeeds in four of the ten-year series, but fails in drawing the designs from memory, and in the reading and report tests. In both of these tests, failures were due largely to the fact that she did not examine the drawings carefully when they were exposed to her view for ten seconds. She pushed the card away after she had gazed at it for four seconds, saying that she could draw them. However, the examiner made her look at them for ten seconds. She then drew the more difficult of the drawings very easily, but could not recall how the simpler one was made. With the reading and report tests, failure was due to her inability to recall the minimum number of items necessary to receive credit. At year twelve she succeeded in all tests, with the exception of the ball and field. On the fourteenth year she failed at the differences between President and King, but succeeded with the remaining tests of this this year. At year sixteen she had four successes, but she failed on the vocabulary test, and the interpretation of fables. At the eighteenth year level she succeeded in repeating eight digits in the order given by the examiner, and seven digits in reverse order.

It is interesting to note that the largest number of delinquents belong to a race which is of an entirely different racial constitution than that of the Anglo-Saxon. That race has a civilization behind it ; it has accomplished great things in art and literature ; it has, indeed, enriched civilization with art and science, and it was marked for its progress during the periods of recuperation after the dark Middle Ages. However, in spite of that it is a people which has never been assimilated by the Anglo-Saxons, to any appreciable extent.

Their views are usually entirely different from the views of the country, so that it is practically impossible for assimilation to be accomplished. In the midst of the great Anglo-Saxon race absorption, they have remained true to their language and habits, to their customs, and only too often they attempt to impose their own primitive tribal laws of revenge and punishment. Their family life is as primitive now as in the years gone by, when the wife was the slave of the family, and when children were an asset for the production of the means of living for the parents. The paterfamilias enforces his absolute rules upon the members of the family, and they have the antiquated views of child-training of their own country.

It is with no intention of race disparagement that I make these observations, for they are all honest and good people, but the true fact is, they are unable to assimilate.

The second racial unit forms another large group of our immigrants. This race has the potentiality of adaptation to any other race, for in the veins of this race courses the blood of every other race on the earth. Centuries of persecution and plunder by the domineering races of the world, under the ægis of the cross or otherwise, they have been forced into racial mixing, and, at the same time, they were segregated by the others. We find among them Mongols, Slavs, Latins and Teutons; and yet they have preserved their religious concept in the face of all adversities. There is no doubt that this perseverance was due to the fact that assimilation was not permitted, that they have been segregated, and that the more the abuse, the stronger the awakening of the racial egotism. However, in this country, they underwent a great amount of assimilation, until two decades ago, when suddenly an awakening of racial consciousness took place by the advent of a large influx of another group of the same race. The religious conflict of the children born of this race is so acute that it is impossible to reconcile it with Anglo-Saxon views. It is clearly seen why the first step of the delinquent is the departure from his own race, the denial of his race and religion. The greatest misfortune of that race is the creation of ghettos, which is incompatible with race assimilation. They live in this country, creating an atmosphere approaching that of their own province. Except for the necessity of coming in contact with the social organization at large, they maintain their own habits and customs, but owing to their great potentiality of adjustment they modify them to a certain extent, though they preserve the fundamentals of their own.

It is in this way that we must look at the problem of environment, and the influence it has in the moulding of the child's personality. I have shown above that the success in adjustment depends not only in the fact that the child must possess the potentiality for that adjustment, but also that the first environmental factor, the family, should be in complete adjustment with the social organization at large.

The case of F. is instructive in that respect. She was nineteen years old when she committed her first offence, and was arrested as an incorrigible a short while after. Her parents were foreign born and came here many years before, bringing with them a large family, all children under eight years of age, with the exception of this girl, who was born in this country. They were respectable people, perfectly well adjusted to the environment of their own country, but adversities in life and financial losses determined their emigration to America. They established themselves amidst the people of their new home town, and for years they there preserved their own ideals and conceptions. The child was born in poverty, but soon after the father succeeded in business and established a well paying enterprise. Of the eight children, only four remained, and all of them, except the delinquent one, succeeded fairly well, attended school, and became interested either in business or professions. The delinquent was the only girl, and the youngest in the family. Before starting to attend school, she was ignorant of the language of this country, but her contact with the street life in her community made her master of an idiom which is common in the neighbourhood. Her home life was pleasant, from her standpoint. Her parents were now in affluent circumstances, and the fact that she was the only girl and the youngest child gave her a position of superiority in the family. Whatever the parents had denied the other children, they were able to give her. They were anxious to dress her better than the other children, and for a short time they had a tutor for her. They gave her music lessons, permitted her enjoyments, and were anxious to see her excel over the other children in the community. They acquired a polish, began to neglect religious ritual, and were careless about the religious instruction of the children in general and the girl in particular. They acquired a misconception of what constituted Americanism. They soon moved from their old district into another, where the people were " cleaner " and " more civilized ", more " American ". From the notes gathered, it appears that the child in question was somewhat different from the others in the family. In the first place, she had a " temper ", and was " different from the others in her desires ". She was stubborn ; putting it more correctly, it appears that she was self-assertive and egocentric. The parents confessed that this characteristic of the child made them give in to her quite often, and they did not care to cross her. It is conceivable that the result was a feeling of powerfulness and egotism. The patient, herself, told me that she could have all she wished, just for the asking. She regarded her parents as old-fashioned people, who did not understand the new ways of life, and she grew up to school life with that view. Around her revolved the entire world.

Her school life was also interesting. She was unable to conceive of others having the same rights as her own, and was unable to perceive that the pain she suffered under certain circumstances would cause pain to others, under similar circumstances. She came in daily conflict with the other children. She did good work in school, but caused annoyance to the teachers through being quarrelsome and disobedient She never displayed sympathy and never felt sorry. She was very untruthful, and her parents were only too ready to complain about the teacher, and the occasional rebuffs she would get in school. She graduated from public school and entered high school with a feeling of superiority. Her parents claimed they could do nothing with her, that she was a good girl, but disobedient and uncontrollable. She cowed the entire household ; she considered her parents ignorant, and her brothers as backward as her parents, who could not understand the girl of to-day. She occasionally stole small change from her family, but never from strangers. She began to play truant, and with the onset of menstruation she left school and refused to return. It was at this time that delinquency started. At the age of fifteen she was a full grown woman, had had sexual experiences, and was in the habit of staying out at night with a young man. She finally took up a business course, and then became acquainted with a married man who promised to marry her as soon as he obtained a divorce from his wife. She lived with him a few days, and during these few days she met his wife, quarrelled with her, begged her to free the husband, and became generally a nuisance. During all this time she denied her religion, claimed to be a Catholic, and, when arrested, she finally admitted her racial origin. She had no respect for her parents, blamed them for her troubles and for not having helped her to keep the man. She blamed the wife for being so ignorant as to interfere with her happiness. Mentally, she was above the average, was co-operative, and answered questions readily. She was somewhat ashamed of her situation, and resented that she should be examined about her mentality when she knew that she was far more intelligent than other girls of her age. She also resented being classed among others far inferior to her. She did not acknowledge the wrong done, and did not regret it. She only wondered how people could be so backward as to misunderstand a girl of her age and ambition.

This case is illustrative of the problem. There is no question that a normal girl would have developed a perfectly well-adjusted personality had the family life been of a somewhat different calibre. In the first place, we have a mal-adjusted family, a family which, though living in our midst, has never become one of us. Then we have the nursing of an egotism (which probably in this instance was overstrong), with no attempt to curb it, and with no attempt to adjust the child to the surroundings. The great conflict in life for that girl was due to the fact that the first stepping-stone to social adjustment was mistakenly undertaken. Her life was ruined, because the family which attempted to assimilate itself to the atmosphere did not do so on account of ignorance as to what assimilation really meant. She was entirely unable to establish a social rapport when she came out in life, and her aim was only self-gratification as dictated by egotism.[1]

[1] Examination : Physical examination was negative, except upper teeth spaced, high narrow palate and slightly enlarged thryoid. She had marked growth of hair over the upper lip and some on the chin. She was of short stature and inclined to obesity. No history of venereal disease.

Equally interesting is another delinquent, representing another group. Her parents were foreign born, and came to this country when she was three years old. During her life in this country she lived continuously within the same few blocks, among people of her own race. It was a typical foreign colony, where the people spoke their foreign tongue, had their weekly religious street festivals, bought imported groceries from their home country, and lived a life similar to that of their country or province. The parents never acquired the language of this country. They were superstitious,

The girl cried a great deal during the examination on account of the treachery of the man, who had lied to her concerning the divorce. She had no insight into the whole affair, did not seem to regret the occurrence, and could not see exactly how a woman is wrong if she lives with the husband of another woman, as long as they love each other. Moreover, she could not understand how a man can lie.

During the examination she passed from crying to laughter with much ease, and declared that she felt very much hurt at being brought to a hospital for examination. She promised that she would never go back to that man. She was not much concerned about the pain she had caused her parents. Religious matters never occupied her head, and she was not much concerned about the spiritual aspect of the affair.

Mental Test :
        Terman Score—16 years, 7 months.
        Intelligence Quotient—1.04
        Interpretation : Average Intelligence.

Details : She obtained a mental age of sixteen years and seven months, with an intelligence quotient of 1.04. This places the patient in the average group. She was upset because she was obliged to take the mental examination, and at the beginning frequently said to herself, " how degrading ", or " how disgraceful ". She co-operated well, because she was anxious to make a good impression and attain a high score. She spoke freely about herself, stating that she felt that her family did not wish her to be at home. She does not consider that she has done anything wrong in going with this married man, who is a friend of hers. The only thing that she is ashamed of is the fact that she is obliged to remain now with girls whom she considers her inferiors, both intellectually and socially. She adds that she does not have to work for a living, but does so merely to keep her mind occupied. She is very sensitive, and twice during the examination she burst into tears because she considered herself humiliated by being brought to the hospital for an examination.

Her basal age was XIV (her real age 19). She succeeded in all the XVI year tests, with the exception of the vocabulary. At year XVIII she was able to repeat eight digits in the order given by the examiner, but failed in the remaining tests of that year.

believed in witchcraft, magic, evil eye, ghosts and the like. They never attended school, and were it not for compulsory education their children would not have attended school. From an early age the girl took work in a nearby shop, and did embroidery at home, helping the family by the old sweat-shop method, the earnings being turned over to the parents. When she started her school life, she was a stranger to the concepts which were being forced upon her. She was not brilliant in school; in fact, she was very dull, played truant a great deal, and was kept at home frequently, in order to help her mother. But there was one thing which filtered into her brain as soon as her school life started. She desired freedom. She wanted to get away from the boredom of family life, resented the punishment meted out to her by her father, and began to yearn for a life away from her parents. Her first sexual experiences took place, at the age of ten, with a boarder in the home. She soon became promiscuous with the boys in the neighbourhood, and at the age of fourteen she left home and went to live with a young man. She was finally arrested as a prostitute.

In this case we see the sharp contrast between the environment at home, and the social organization at large. However, when the child came to face the outside world, the contrast between the two environments was so great that the conflict ended disastrously for the girl. Of course, in addition to this very important factor, there were other factors which were significant and which will be discussed later.

The rôle played by environment can also be seen from a consideration of another group of cases. I refer to those cases where the parents have died, and the child is put under the care of strangers. It is important to recall, here, those few remarks made about heredity being a continuation of growth, and I added then, " not only physical, but also psychical ". The child of two people (father and mother) will possess not only the physical characteristics of the parents, but also the psychical. The child is also born with a potentiality to reach the psychical development of the parents, and, as a matter of fact, to overreach their development. That potentiality is the basis which makes progress possible. There is no doubt that there is a psychical rapport present between the parents and the child, because there is that biological continuity present. Primarily, the child possesses the potentiality of adaptability to the family life of the parents, and to the moral concepts of the family, on account of heredity. The possibility of adaptation to the social organization at large takes place only after harmony has been established between child and family. However, to a family of strangers, with which the child has nothing but racial traits in common, the process of adaptation is more difficult and frequently impossible. This is, to my mind, the reason for the numerous failures in the bringing up of wards, or of children placed under the care of strangers. From the many cases of that sort under my observation, it will be interesting to note one here. It is the history of a girl of seventeen, who could be classed as a wayward minor, but, through the intelligence of the people who brought her up, has so far escaped being in conflict with the law. I mention this case because I had an opportunity to confer with the people and social workers, and also to have a lengthy conversation with the girl herself. Her case was very well known to me.

W., seventeen years of age, was born in America,

from unknown parents. She was an abandoned child, and was brought up for the first few months of her life in a hospital. When she was eight months old a young couple presented themselves, who were anxious to adopt her. They had just lost a daughter, after a serious illness, and decided not to attempt to have other children of their own. They had a boy of a little over a year, but they wanted a girl. After an investigation, the child was given to them for adoption. They moved into a different city, as they wanted to bring the child up as their own, and for the years following she seemed to be their own. At no time did the child know the truth of her parentage, neither did their own little boy. She was a bright little girl, intelligent, but over-egotistic. The parents indulged her more than the boy; they were afraid to deny her things, in order to impress upon themselves that she was their own. The result was that she had the run of things. She grew up selfish, egocentric and full of faults. She was showered with affection, with love which frequently was not genuine, but conscious and intentional. The adoptive mother was afraid of a guilty conscience. However, she noticed that the child did not act as their own, and could not be as their own; there was a great difference in every way between their boy and the girl. A rapport was never established. The secret which the parents kept so very well hidden for sixteen years was finally revealed to the girl by a former neighbour of her adopted parents, whom she met by chance.

She left home and had soon forgotten the affection of her foster parents. They were strangers to her; she had no affection for them. Now she understood why she could never adapt herself to their ways, why she always felt different, why she was never really like a daughter to the woman who had brought her up.[1]

This short history is instructive in that it shows that a proper adaptation never took place in the family life, that the first environment of the child's life was entirely impossible, and that, in consequence the tendency of that family life was to increase the egotism of the child.

There is another group in my material, which it is important to mention ; that is the patient whose parents were living, but who, on account of the parents' moral turpitude, was taken out of their home and put under the care of strangers or a relative. Then there is the girl who is taken over by relatives on account of the extreme poverty of her own parents. In both of these types the children were older ; as a rule, they have reached the school age, and the first impressions were made at home. Moreover, such children were frequently taken back by the parents and then again left their home. The home atmosphere was immoral, as a rule alcoholism was the chief vice. The strangers who took the children, or the relatives, were never selected with care, and in one instance the aunt who took a child was in a worse moral state than the parents. It should also not be forgotten that these children were a product of people below par mentally, morally and emotionally. As a matter of fact, all were mentally below par, being either in the moron group, or distinct imbeciles. Not only did they show the stigmata of degeneration, but also the traces of corruption due to an unhealthy moral atmosphere. We could safely call such an environment disorganized, disintegrating, degenerate. There was nothing which would help to train, mould or shape a personality. Egotism was rampant ; it was supported

---

[1] The intelligence co-efficient was 1.14.

and glorified, but it was the egotism approaching that of the animal, namely, self-satisfaction, self-gratification, and a continuous desire for pleasures of the bestial kind. From this group we obtain the prostitutes, as a rule.

In analysing my material, I distinguished two other groups which are important to mention here, for the environment involved was quite different.

In the first group, the mother was the only one living, and she was usually forced to work and support the family. The father died when the child was very young, and there were other children. As far back as these children can remember, there was always want. In fact, there was no family life. The neighbours took care of the children during the day, and often they would roam around the streets, fending for themselves. The school life was irregular ; there were no means of supervising the actions of the children, and only too often the street boys took advantage of them. The conditions were even worse, where the mother died and left the father alone with the children. These children became a prey to every conceivable mishap, and sooner or later they were used as tools by gangsters or other disreputable characters.

It is interesting to note the two outstanding facts in the lives of these girls, the onset of puberty and the first sexual experience. Before puberty there was nothing reproachable about the girls. The characteristics were those of an overstrong egotism, but the children were docile, and, to a certain extent, amenable to training. The emotional instability and delinquency started with the onset of puberty.

The first sexual experience had the same effect. It would appear that every moral stronghold was lost with that, for shame and all that goes to make up strength of character was destroyed, and life was thrown suddenly into channels without concern for right and wrong.

It is this raw material, the product of either mal-adjusted or immoral personalities, that forms the bulk of our delinquents. As raw material, they enter school to be moulded into adjusted social units, into desirable personalities, and then return home, until the next schoolday, to the same atmosphere of degeneracy or maladjustment. What one year of school life attempts to accomplish is destroyed by a few days of home life. The primary stepping-stone being defective, the second can be of little avail.

III

THE MAKE-UP

The Concept of Constitutional Inferiority

It is impossible to take up the study of delinquency without delving at length into the subject of mental defectiveness. For a long period of time, the main preoccupation of criminologists and psychologists was to show the close relationship between the two states. Mental retardation was, of course, usually regarded as the basis upon which a defective personality was built up. Kraepelin, for one, in his study of criminals, came to that conclusion.[1] On the other hand, others made that mental defectiveness an actual cause of of delinquency, and only in this way could we conceive the conclusion which Bleuler reached, that " the criminal as reo nato is the rule."[2]

We notice here an attempt to reconcile the old theory of the individual born with a moral defect, and the newer conception of environmental influences upon an individual born with the moral defect. This attempt at conciliation between the two conceptions led the famous German criminal lawyer, F. v. List, to define the criminal as " a product of the intrinsic constitution of the criminal himself, of *an individual* factor and many social factors." [3]

[1] Kauffmann, M. : *Psychologie des Verbrechens*, 1912, p. 28.

[2] Bleuler, E. : *Der Geborene Verbrecher*, p. 33.

[3] Hirsch, Paul : *Verbrechen und Prostitution als Soziale Krankheitserscheinungen*, p. 22.

F

The actual study of mental defectiveness and delinquency or criminality has been taken up seriously in
America and England. Conclusions vary greatly, as
will be shown later, and public opinion, is, as yet, not
in a receptive mood for the admission that many
offenders are below par mentally. To the layman, they
appear normal; the ordinary social relations give the
offenders a sufficient amount of cleverness, of adroitness,
to be able to move around in life, and they only show
their mental deficiency when confronted with situations
which are out of their daily routine. They then show
their lack of resourcefulness, and have difficulty in getting
out of painful situations. In general, when the actions
concerned refer to the primitive instinct of self-preservation, they are at a disadvantage in concealing their
innate mental backwardness. They will often show
a great amount of resourcefulness when it comes to
reaching an aim to satisfy their ego, to revenge an injustice done them, or to rid themselves of painful situations. But their resourcefulness is most of the time
puerile in accomplishment; there is always a flaw in
their plans, and at the last moment there is a flaw which
condemns the entire plan to failure. That can be easily
verified by studying the offences committed by delinquents. Those offences are often so simple-minded,
and there are so many faults in the performance, that
it is no wonder they fail. It is their peculiarity that
they never take the shortest route towards the solution
of a problem. Their route is devious, with many zig-
zags and changes in the plans, on account of their
emotional instability and their susceptibility to various
stimuli.

However, we do not rely simply on the study of
their actions in order to form an opinion of their

mentality. The interesting report of Dr. V. V. Anderson, in his summary on the " Juvenile-Court-Survey Cases " [1] mentions the fact that fully fifty per cent. of the children were rated as backward, subnormal, border-line, or mentally defective. Out of this total 9.2 per cent. were suffering from neuroses, 8.6 per cent were psycho-pathic personalities, and only 3.2 per cent. were definitely feeble-minded. The other 174 children were, to all intents and purposes, as measured by the various mental tests, of a normal intelligence.

These findings are practically identical with those of other investigators and help to dispel the usual assertion that all delinquents are mentally backward.

These data are by no means left without contradiction. The conclusions drawn by some workers are that the greatest number of delinquents (some authors say 80 per cent.) are mental defectives.[2] From all these reports, the outstanding thought is that delinquency and mental retardation are in very close relationship. The difference of opinion rests, unquestionably, upon the difference of interpretation of the findings with mental measurements. Burt calls attention to this very fact[3] and takes occasion to throw considerable doubt upon American results.

However, the fact that a great many delinquents are mentally below par does not, by any means, explain delinquency. There are certainly many more mental defectives who are not delinquents. Mental defectiveness by itself may be a very great contributory factor, but it is not a deciding factor. Moreover, there are a great number of morons who are useful citizens, and there

[1] Anderson, V. V.: l.c. p. 39.

[2] *Third Annual Report of Probation Office*, Cook County, Illinois, 1914.

[3] Burt, Cyril: l.c. p. 285.

are yet more so-called border-line persons who are evidently successful in life.

Yet, in spite of all these facts, it cannot be denied that delinquency and mental retardation go hand-in-hand.

Three hundred delinquent girls classified according to the mental test gave the following results :

Average Mentality	61
Border-line	76
Morons	107
Dullards	53
Psychotic (Definite Psychosis or Undifferentiated Psychosis)	3

In the group "average mentality" we include a few of superior intelligence, others of average and others of low average. Many of the so-called "border-line" would be included by some authors as low average, so that 137 girls can be taken out of the group of mental defectives. It means, therefore, that only a little over fifty per cent. of my delinquents were definitely mentally retarded, which coincides with the views of Dr. Anderson. I also included, in my group of defectives, the three psychotic girls, as they were definitely mentally retarded in addition to the psychosis.

From this group of 300 delinquents, I selected a smaller group of thirty in order to compare the results obtained by the mental tests applied to them with those obtained by other means. The correlation of the various facts about those thirty delinquents was highly significant, and one appeared as a logical sequence to another. Out of thirty girls selected, five were charged with petty larceny, twelve with prostitution, twelve with waywardness and incorrigibility, and one with abandonment of her baby. The last girl would not have been included in this group, if abandonment had been the only charge, but she was arrested, originally, for prostitution.   These three groups of girls represent the three classes of delinquent girls, each distinct from the other.   The nature of their offences is such, and the relationship between those offences and the mental status is so intimate, that they may be regarded as three distinct groups.   In character and emotional make-up, in emotional stability, and other features a well as heredity, they are distinctly different from each other.   Especially the class of the wayward girls is one far removed from the other two.   Out of these thirty girls, only five gave the result of " average mentality ". The highest intelligence co-efficient obtained among these five was 1.04, and the lowest was .95.   All of them were from the class of waywards and all were first offenders.

The following table can be set up, showing the results obtained with the girls selected :

Average mentality	5
Border-line	8
Morons	10
Dullards	6
Psychopathic	1

From a study of the rest of my material the results are about the same ;   the girls classed as first offenders and waywards gave a higher intelligence quotient than the others.   Of course, there were some in that group who gave a very low mental test, but, as a rule, those girls were guilty of offences of a more serious nature, for which, however, there was insufficient legal evidence. Their past history was also more significant ;   they were recidivists and were, at one time, put on probation

by the Children's Court. Their arrest was more a pre-
ventive measure, either on the demand of the parents
or guardians (the latter, as a rule, the probation officer).

The result of a mental test is a co-efficient obtained
by comparing the mentality of the person tested and
that of a child at a certain age. When the result, for
example, shows a mental age of six years, it means that
the person in question has the mental faculties of a
six-year-old child. However, this co-efficient has only
a relative, apparent value. There is less similarity
between the mentality of a child and a delinquent
than is usually supposed. In the first place, the child
of six shows a mentality which is normal for that age ;
the problems that confront the child at that age are
easy for him to solve, and when put in more difficult
situations, there is that reserve mentality, and that
potentiality of adaptation of the normal organism which
will make the brain work, and after a short time extricate
itself out of the difficulties. It is otherwise with the
delinquent. He may be able to answer the questions
and the problems of the six-year-old child, but if put
in the same difficulties as the child, the absence of innate
potentiality of adjustment will show itself. He is, in
fact, more handicapped on account of the greater number
of varied stimuli and experiences during a longer life,
which made him unable to direct himself properly and
harmoniously. For example, it is a well-known fact
that lying is a characteristic of childhood. Of course,
there are children who do not lie, and I have personal
knowledge of such children, but even those children,
when it is a question of protecting the ego, will also
have recourse to lying. The child suspected by his
parents or by the teacher of committing an infraction,
when it is a question of saving itself from a reprimand

or punishment, will, if he does not tell a lie, at least try to get out of the difficulty by giving an excuse, or he will fabricate an excuse, based upon plausible evidences. This so-called plausible fabrication is quite characteristic of childhood. The fabrication will possess many elements of probability, trivial truthful incidents will be inter-woven, and recourse will be had to witnesses who may at that time have been in the neighbourhood, or being sympathetically inclined to the particular child, will probably support his story. That is the way with the child.

The delinquent is also a liar, a prevaricator, a fabricator of imaginary occurrences. But his lies are fantastic, without the probability of truth, without the semblance of possible truth. They are puerile in the sense that they are lies, but they are ludicrous; they are very often pitifully ridiculous. Their stories are frequently contradictory, and when the attention of the delinquent is called to this, he or she will still maintain it, or not answer at all; will appear surprised, and then maintain it again. It is the refuge of a simple mind to say the first thing which may suggest itself, but without foresight of substantiation, without thought of possible questions which may arise. The child's mind is logical, able to draw conclusions, to put together facts; the feeble-minded, on the other hand, acts without logic, and only too frequently without a semblance of logic.

The case of R. is illustrative of this point: A girl of sixteen, arrested as a wayward minor, but as a matter of fact an addict to petty larceny for which she was once on probation, claimed that she was chased out of the house by her father on account of not being able to get along with her step-mother. Her father, though addicted to alcohol, had a good reputation in the neighbourhood ; her step-mother was a woman above reproach. The delinquent was often in trouble. As a school child she was arrested for playing truant, for immorality and for petty larceny. A charge of improper guardianship was placed against the father, but the case was dismissed. She was a troublesome girl all through her childhood. After she left school she was arrested for compulsory prostitution, but she was unable to prove her case against the men, and was put on probation. She rarely worked, was lazy and impudent. The story of her last offence was told by the girl, as follows : After a quarrel with her step-mother, her father told her to leave the house. It was in the evening, and as she had no place to go, she wandered up and down the street. After a while, she decided to go up on the roof of the house where her father conducted a grocery store, wait there until he should close the store, and then steal into the apartment (which was in the same house) and go to sleep. Two boys saw the girl go up on the roof, and followed her. They assaulted her there and then dragged her down the stairway and out into the street. During this entire time, she screamed, but no one came to help her. The boys dragged her along the street until they reached an apartment house, then dragged her to an apartment, and kept her there against her will.[1]

[1] Examination : The general physical examination was negative.
Mental Examination :

> Age : 16 years, 7 months, 19 days.
> Terman Score : 11 years, 2 months.
> Intelligence Quotient : .70

This quotient places the patient on the dividing line between the feeble-minded and border-line groups. There was a great deal about her work which suggested that she had had the test before, but she denied this. She co-operated well and seemed anxious to please.
Her basal age is IX years. Tests of the VIII year resulted in

In checking up her story, the impossibility of the entire occurrence was seen immediately. It would have been impossible to have dragged her through the hall-way of the house, because she would have passed her own apartment. The house where this is supposed to have happened is one of the crowded houses in the poorer section of the city where there is a continuous stream of people in the street, and in and out of the houses. She finally admitted the untruth of many of her statements, and concluded by saying that the story as told by her was a fabrication.

The frequent statement by various offenders, when caught in the act of committing the offence, that they were innocent, but that someone else gave them the article to hold for them for a few minutes, is also often heard, in spite of the palpable lie attached to it. A young man was arrested early in the morning, while carrying a bundle of dry goods from a store which was burglarized only a few hours before. He stated that he was walking peacefully towards his own home, when two strangers accosted him. The strangers told him to keep the parcels they had, inasmuch as they could not use the things in the parcels, and wished to get rid of them. He did not open the parcels, and was ignorant of their contents. Somewhat similar was the story of a girl whom I examined. She was put on probation for waywardness and incorrigibility, and the probation officer found a position for her as a maid. For the first few weeks she was satisfactory, but soon she disappeared, and with her also

success. She succeeded in all the X year groups, except the vocabulary, her score being twenty-eight of the necessary thirty. In the XII year she succeeded in the definitions of abstract words, ball and field problem, dissected sentences and the repetition of 5 digits reversed. She failed in all the XIV year group, except giving differences between President and King. Her upper limit is the average adult series.

some small articles of jewellery. She returned, after a few days, to the probation officer, telling her that some one had given her the articles, and that she had found out that they belonged to the family she worked for. She therefore came to return the articles.

As noted in all the stories told by the delinquents who are mentally backward, we find incoherence in the entire matter, and the absence of any logical sequence in the story.

Another characteristic of the delinquent is the desire for notoriety. During the questioning, very few show any embarrassment or prudery. They are not depressed, except when it is for the purpose of making an impression. They assume poses which are usually copied from various screen beauties they have seen. They are glad to have an opportunity to show themselves off, and are overcome by the chance of being the centre of attraction. I have often heard them argue points of law, trying to show how versed they are in matters of that kind, and trying hard to convince one they are not as simple as they are taken to be. They smile and then cry ; they are insistent most of the time that they know their rights. That is a characteristic of this type of girl. They are happy when their pictures appear in the daily papers, and when a short description is given of them and their case. They are all vain, and vanity is the chief trait of their souls.

But the dangerous type is the girl with an average mental test, the one who possesses sufficient native ability to think logically and to frame a sequence of ideas and occurrences. They are impudent and insulting when they are dealing with a sentimental man or woman on the bench. They are sufficiently clever to slip by the scrutiny of the law. Equal to this excessive vanity and desire for notoriety is their weakness to flattery. They are an easy prey to that. Flattery is the best method of approach. We find it also in children, except that they attach to it more importance. I have so far failed to see a delinquent who did not like flattery. It is this characteristic which makes them easy prey to the gangster, to the moral degenerate and to the exploiter of women.

I have frequently tried to find out how many delinquents whom I have examined regretted their predicament, and felt sorry for the pain they had caused to themselves and to their families. Out of fifty girl delinquents whom I questioned with that idea in mind, only two showed real regret and felt deeply sorry for the entire affair. It is interesting to note that, in this respect, all the delinquents, irrespective of their mental age, were more or less alike. Some of them at first appeared to feel sorry and to show real emotional distress, but immediately afterwards they would declaim a tirade against the parents, saying as quickly as before that it was " nobody's business what they did."

G., for example, was a very intelligent girl of nineteen, who was arrested by her brother as a wayward. She gave a very high mental age, was a high school and business school graduate, and while working occupied good paying and responsible positions. But her home life was marked by frequent quarrels with the other members of the family, on account of religious matters and on account of the fact that her parents protested about her going out so often and spending most of the evenings in cabarets. She finally left home, in the company of a married man, whose private life was scandalous, and who, at that time, was on probation for non-support of his wife. During the examination she appeared to feel sorry for the heartaches that she had brought to her mother, and admitted that the man was not worth her troubles, and that she was far superior to him. When she was asked, " Why did you leave a home of comfort and happiness and cause so much anguish to your people, to go and live with a man who has a wife and children, and who is very poor and could under no circumstances give you the same comfort that you had at home ", she answered, after a while, bursting into tears, " I never thought of that ". But immediately, when her attention was called to the quarrels with her parents on account of her religious differences of opinion, she began to talk against her family, using very insulting language, and blaming them for her trouble. " No, I don't feel sorry for them." And that was the amount of regret she showed about the entire affair.

It has frequently been said that all delinquents love gang life, and that they are always together in groups. The same has also been said about feeble-minded individuals. As a matter of fact, this is not so, when analysed carefully. Even in their school life they are seclusive, their association with other children is out of necessity and circumstance, not because their soul yearns for associates. They have very few friends, and those friends are mostly girls or boys who impose themselves upon them for various purposes. They do not entrust their plans to others ; they have no ideas suitable to be so entrusted. Only impulsively they will tell something, and follow, as a rule, the advice given them at the time, unless other stimuli arise which may change their plans.

But all these characteristics are the outcome of ego-tism, are dictated by egotism and are determined in their course by egotism. Indeed, the delinquents are egotists, and unsurpassable egotists. They may occasionally show love and affection to their parents, but at the same time—one reprimand, and they forget all the love and affection and turn against them. Or what is more important, any attempt to curb the ego in its rampant way will stir them up and they will take a course, which, at the end, will lead to their destruction.

How are we going to express the fundamental make-up of the delinquent? To say that every delinquent is mentally feeble, would mean to contradict the true findings, inasmuch as there are delinquents who are not mentally feeble. Of course, the latter show characteristics which approach the subnormal, but not from the standpoint of the Intelligence Test. Then, of course, there are numerous individuals who are mentally feeble, and are not delinquents. There are, therefore, other psychological characteristics which are of importance, which are more responsible for their subsequent development into delinquents, and those characteristics must be of fundamental importance. Moreover, we discover, in the analysis of the delinquents, that in childhood it was not their low mentality which brought them to the attention of other people, but something different, a characteristic which is often called " a queer twist ", a peculiarity which distinguished them from other children. When brought to the physician, these children were diagnosed as " nervous ", as " temperamental ". The school-teacher called them " impossible, obnoxious ", etc. At work, later in life, they were called " lazy, inattentive and useless ". Few of them ever graduated from school; most of them left school at a late age, to go to work, and never reached the higher classes. I have often wondered why some of these children were ever promoted from class to class, and the reply given by a teacher concerning this was, " that we found it was the only way to get rid of them."

It is, therefore, not so much the mental age which is the important factor, though it undoubtedly plays a very great rôle, but something else, something which forms the main trend of their souls, and which stamps them as psychologically inferior. It is that psychological inferiority which is transmitted at birth as a psychic defect, and which is developed into certain channels leading to delinquency. This inferiority is pre-natal, is congenital. It is this state which is responsible for the absence of the potentiality of adjustment, and it is this, together with the organic inferiority, which represents what is generally known as constitutional inferiority.[1]

We are probably reverting, here, to an opinion which was, to a great extent, a pet theory of past criminologists, the conception that the delinquent is primarily an hereditary product, and secondarily a social product.

However, on closer analysis it can be seen that the hereditary product is not an individual with a delinquent or criminal personality, but an inferior individual, psychologically. The entire psychological entity, which forms what we popularly call the personality of an individual human being, is in this case defective. All the attempts at adjustment to the various social stimuli are fruitless. Such a personality remains a " stranger " amidst this great social organization, and the entire structure of society is, for him, an unintelligible tangle. The institutions of this social structure, with the outgrowth of moral codes, are incomprehensible for such person-alities, who cannot, in the course of a few years, in child-

[1] Cf. chapter on Organic Inferiority.

hood, reach to the stage of assimilation. Delinquency, on the other hand, is a product of environmental factors, when working upon such a personality. I vainly looked for the " criminal type " of an individual. There is no such type, but I was able to detect, after a careful examination and an analysis of the life history of an individual, the type of the constitutional inferior.

A fuller analysis of this will be undertaken in the chapter on " Organic Inferiority".

IV

MOTIVES OF DELINQUENCY

It is characteristic of the child never to admit guilt. After committing an infraction, the child will, as a rule, keep quiet ; then, if possible, try to cover up that infraction by actions which will give it the semblance of an incidental occurrence, which would throw the blame on someone else. But important data on child-psychology are obtained when we observe the child at the time the infraction is discovered and the guilt points towards him. I have rarely met a child who will admit frankly, and without excuses, the wrong done, and the child trained to admit an infraction will, as a rule, attempt to justify it by numerous ingenious excuses. In this respect the delinquent shows similarity to the child. They will invariably find an excuse, no matter how flimsy it is.

In examining delinquent girls, I have always made it my practice to obtain from them information on two points :

First : The motive which prompted them to commit the offence, and secondly, how the offence was committed.

In the second question there was also a third point of importance, namely, how they excused the offence committed, how they justified it, and what view they had about it as "*a wrong committed*." In one word, it was important to learn from them if they had any conception of what is *right* and *wrong*, if they were able to judge similar acts, and what would be their behaviour if they had to pass judgment on similar actions in others. Also, it was interesting to know if they could conceive the idea of a wronged society and of the rights of a community. It is, indeed, easy to talk about an offence punishable by law when the person committing the offence cannot understand that someone has been hurt, and cannot regard that someone concretely. We are, to a certain extent, dealing with abstract ideas, and the delinquent may not be able to comprehend it. For example, I am in possession of notes taken during the examination of a girl accused of prostitution, who could not understand how she had committed a wrong, when no one was hurt by her being a prostitute. It was her own body that she gave, and it did not harm anyone. Of course, the girl accused of petty larceny, like shop lifting, understood readily that she had taken from someone something which did not belong to her ; she had hurt a shopkeeper who had paid for the goods she had stolen, but it was different with a girl who was arrested as a wayward during a raid on a dance hall.

These and similar questions had to be answered before any conclusions could be drawn.

As a rule, the girls could be divided into groups, according to their degree of mentality. The girl giving an intelligence test approaching normal or above normal was an extravagant liar, and her excuses were palpable lies. It was impossible to put any credence in her story, and it could be seen that she had expected the questions. Her story was thought over and over in her mind, and she had told it to the investigator,

G

to the judge and to myself. But some truth could be obtained from time to time.

On the other hand, the girl with an intelligence below par was sincere in her story, and the contradictions were such that she became easily confused, but her answers contained a great deal of psychological truth. I will illustrate the important points as to motives and actions, by various examples :

R., Cloak room girl, twenty-four years old, born in America, of American born parents.

Family : Her father is dead. He was a general labourer and worked in a factory in her home town in Massachusetts. Her mother is living and works in a factory. She has one brother, but very little could be found out about him. No sisters. No information could be obtained about her parents beyond the fact that they were poor people and were factory workers. The patient is married, but nothing could be ascertained concerning her husband, except that he was not living with her.

Past : The childhood of the patient could not be ascertained. She went to public school and graduated, at the age of 14½ years, and then went to work in the same factory where her mother worked. Her employment record at that place is unknown. She married at the age of eighteen and lived with her husband only a short time, then left him, because they could not get along. She came to New York only two months ago, with a woman whom she claims she had met casually, and intended to go to work. This girl had never been in New York before, yet she claims that during these two months she had made many friends. Her story was inconsistent and had so many contradictions that it is evidently untrue. She spoke of trips from New York to Boston, forgetting that she claimed she had been in New York only two months, and that this seems too short a time to allow her to have made so many trips, and to have so many friends.

Present : She claims that one evening she had made an appointment with a girl friend to go to a dance. Knowing that she would have no time to go home for lunch, she left home in the morning, wearing her best dress underneath her working dress. After work she entered a small department store, with no intention of buying anything, but to look around and pass the time until she met her friend. She was arrested in the store, the storekeeper claiming that she had stolen the dress that she was wearing, and she was held for trial. The girl told the story of her arrest as follows : " I entered a dress store, and was looking around for a dress, in order to pass the time while waiting for a friend, when a saleswoman approached and accused me of having stolen a dress. As a matter of fact, I did have two dresses on, one on top of the other, but while the saleswoman claimed that the dress I had on top was the stolen one, I claimed that it was my own dress. It is true that the dress I was accused of stealing was a new one, and was similar to the other dresses on display in the store, but that was a coincidence. I happened to have bought a similar dress in another store. However, I could not remember the store, and I maintain that the tag they found on the dress was not there when I entered ; they probably pinned that tag on while I was waiting to be arrested."

From conversation had with the patient, it was evident that it was not the first time she had been in trouble. Her arguments were mature, and with a definite amount of shrewdness. She was decidedly untruthful, and knew just how much to tell about herself. She was not very much concerned about what happened to her, used language that showed she was acquainted with court procedure, and knew exactly what could happen to her.

Mental examination :

> Age : 24 years, 2 months, 28 days.
> Terman Score : 16 years, 7 months.
> Intelligence Quotient : 1.03.

This quotient places the patient among the average adults. She answers the questions quickly, reasons logically and shows good judgment in reasoning out the answers. Her range of tests is narrow, her basal age occurring at year fourteen. At year sixteen she succeeds in all the tests, with the exception of the code test.

In this test she makes only 2½ errors and she completes it within two minutes and six seconds. Since she was allowed six minutes to complete the test, it is probable that if she had taken more time she would have succeeded in eliminating the errors made. At the eighteenth year level she succeeded in repeating eight digits, but failed in all the other tests of this year, although she endeavoured to work at them.

The subsequent physical examination showed an under-developed patient, pale and anæmic looking. Her voice was low, and she had a peculiar anæmic smile. Her thyroid was palpable, symmetrically enlarged. Her palate was high and narrow, the teeth were spaced, and the skin felt dry. She had a staring look in her eyes, sat smiling during the examination, and answered questions freely and without restraint. She felt perfectly at ease, but her co-operation was only apparent, for it was palpable that her answers were untruthful, that she was an experienced liar, and that she was used to such situations as the one in which she found herself at that time.

Her life up to her arrest, according to her own story, was immoral, not because she was a bad girl, but because she *never thought about it*. On being asked how she came to steal a dress, she denied it flatly, and replied, " Every Saturday night, after work, I go to a dance, and in order not to return home from work and change clothes, I put on my evening dress in the morning, and then I put on my working dress over it. When I am through working, I go to meet my friend ; we eat and then go to the dance hall. There I slip off my old dress and remain in my new one." But, as it happened, the evening dress was on top of the old one, and it was much shorter than the old one, so that it could be seen that she was wearing an old soiled dress underneath a good and new one. When her attention was called to this, she answered, " Did it ? Let me see. Yes, I went to the ladies' room in the store and changed it around." When she was told that all this did not sound plausible, her only reply was " Well."

All these denials came as a matter of course, and at no time did she admit her contradictions. It only appeared to her very strange that her story did not go, and she believed that she would be able to convince the judge about her truthfulness. However, the dress was of no use to her ; it was too small, and too short. It did not fit her. She was not in want, for she was working (the only fact which could be corroborated), and she earned sufficiently to buy herself a dress.

I had similar experiences with all the shop-lifters who came under my observation. I believe that in my cases only two women came to my notice who stole as professional shop-lifters, and I recollect only one instance where a desire to send a present to a child of hers determined a formerly well-to-do woman to steal small items from a department store. In all the other instances the shop-lifters had no reason to steal, either economic (poverty or desire to possess a thing which they could not obtain otherwise), or with some other sort of explanation. They stole out of sheer wickedness, out of disregard for other people's property, on account of the apparent ease with which it seemed to them, they could steal. They stole because it seemed to them so much easier to get a thing for which they would not spend their own earnings, and in that way their earnings would remain for other luxuries which could not be stolen.

I may mention here another shop-lifter, who was thrice convicted, and a few times on probation. It is the story of a woman of forty-five, married, and the mother of two healthy grown-up children. She was arrested for stealing a lampshade in a department store. It was a bulky lampshade, and in addition to that she also stole a small marble statuette. Her husband was in a fairly comfortable position, a good provider, and there was no want in the family. Each time she was caught stealing she had taken some article which could hardly be concealed, and she was caught each time. The excuse she gave was that she could never think of spending money for such things, and yet she wanted the articles.

There is only one class similar to that of the shop-lifter, namely, the pickpocket ; both are petty thieves, and both are untrustworthy.

The other delinquents show an entirely different aspect, especially those giving a low mental test. In none of the delinquents could a plausible excuse for the delinquency be found. The motives given were always absurd or ridiculous, depending upon the degree of mentality of each delinquent. No really adequate excuse was ever offered.

S. was found in a dazed condition in a moving picture house. She gave her age as sixteen, of American birth, Catholic, and coming from a small New England city. She was unable to give more data about herself, claimed that she did not remember her address, or the names of her parents or relatives. She remembered only that she was out with some men, and that she lived with them, but how she reached New York, or how she came into that theatre she did not remember. On examination, the most striking thing was that her language was far from being correct English, and that her facial appearance classed her immediately as a Jewess. She was able to talk Jewish freely, and perfectly, and she knew nothing about Christianity. She wore a small cross around her neck, and she called herself by a well-known American name. After a while she broke down and admitted that she was Jewish, that she never was in New England, and that her age was fourteen. She was unable to give any explanation for her conduct, and none could be obtained.

Her home life, as ascertained later, was happy, her parents were comfortably situated, and there was no want. She was a public school pupil, and there was no reason for her leaving home. On the other hand, her misbehaviour with young men in the neighbourhood was common gossip. She was admonished frequently by her parents, but there was no punishment, corporal or otherwise.

Very frequently we find the statement made by

writers and speakers, that the main cause for young girls leaving home is a disagreement between parents and girl. As a rule, there is a current opinion that the parents mistreat the girl, make her life unbearable, shock her moral sense, making her leave home.   She decides to run away and look for a quiet and happy life. I have only too often encountered · girls where the treatment at home was far from good, where brutality was a daily occurrence, and where there was no liberty, but constant drudgery.   At first, this is exactly the story the girl will tell, and the very sympathetic social worker agrees and pities the girl. With this view in mind, I have tried to find out if that was really one of the important reasons, and how much truth there was in it. I will give here an illustrative case, which represents an entire group.

M., eighteen years of age, American born of foreign born parents. Her father, a citizen for the past twenty years, and an American resident for the past thirty years, scarcely speaks English. He is a plain labourer of low grade intelligence. Her mother, who has been in America for the past twenty-five years, does not speak English. The father is a moderate drinker, and is known to have a bad temper. The mother is quick tempered, but otherwise normal. The girl graduated from public school. The mental test showed her to be dull, giving an intelligence quotient of .84. She co-operated well, and considered the test below her dignity. Her manners suggested that she was paying a great deal of attention to the impression she might be making during the examination.

The girl stated that she ran away from home, because her parents were too strict with her. This strictness was relaxed in the case of her younger brother and sister

She believed that they were trying to make a home girl out of her. She left home and went to live with a girl friend, and there she was assaulted by a friend of the other girl. She lived with the man for a time, and later found out that her mother was ill, so she went home. Her mother insisted that she undergo a physical examination. For fear of that she ran away again, and was then arrested.

According to the investigation, the strictness of the parents consisted in the fact that they objected to the numerous male friends of a disreputable character who were taking the girl out, and also objected to her staying out late at night. During the examination the girl was bitter against her parents, and she refused to tell the name of the man who lived with her. She claimed that she was not " yellow ", that she would not " squeal ", and used a great deal of slang. One of her expressions was : " I can lay my finger on him whenever I want to, and in five or six years more, after I establish myself in the business world, I intend to let him suffer for this."

In all the cases where the so-called ill-treatment at home forced girls to leave, and when, through unforeseen circumstances, they begin to go downward, there is one outstanding feature. In the first place, it was a trifle which made them leave home, and, in the second place, they were so at one with the disintegrating home atmosphere that it is unbelievable that this was the cause for leaving. Then it must also be considered that, with very few exceptions, they never leave home for some better situation. On the contrary, they go to much worse conditions. The outstanding point was, that whenever they left home, it was for an atmosphere devoid of supervision, where all their suppressed desires and instincts could have full sway, and where there was no censor.

There is another reason which writers on the subject make responsible for the delinquency of girls, and that is the economic factor. Only too often the assertion is made that poverty will drive a woman to prostitution and shop-lifting, petty larceny, and all-round bad behaviour. Then we have the frequent assertion that a home atmosphere where want is a daily occurrence, where the absence of the daily necessities are great, will be responsible for the making of a delinquent, especially for her leaving home. Then also the girl who is brought up in poverty, envious of the other girls who have nice things in life, will leave home and seek adventure.

There is, of course, a semblance of truth in all these statements, but only an apparent truth, which is dispelled as soon as the matter is investigated. It is necessary, when the above assertions are made, to prove that the girls leaving home had a definite plan in mind, that their leaving home was determined by that plan, and that after leaving home they showed an attempt to follow a path which might, under lucky circumstances, lead towards a betterment of their condition. But the investigation proved the contrary. It showed that no girl left home with a definite plan in mind, and that they did not know where they were going. Of course, there are exceptions, but these belong definitely to the group of delinquents, and the path taken by them was also different. I will give, here, a history of a case which is representative of a group—the prostitute girl combined with the offence of petty larceny. As a rule, a girl who is a prostitute will very often also be a shop-lifter.

S., sixteen years old, born in Scotland, and only

a little over a year in America. Her intelligence quotient was fifty-eight, which placed her among the distinctly feeble-minded. Her family history was not commendable. Her father was an alcoholic, and her mother was feeble-minded. One sister, who came to this country some years before, was once arrested for prostitution and could not at the time be located. Her personal past history showed that she had lost her position as a clerk in a department store on account of insubordination and carelessness. She could find other work, but was lazy, and then " prostitution was much easier, and it was associated with a merry life." Her reason for shop-lifting was novel. She claimed " that the store where I committed the offence owed me a week's wages, and when I came for my money I was told that I did not work regularly and came late, and therefore they intended to deduct some money. I took the money they gave me, and went into the store with the idea of revenge. I had a perfect right to steal the article, which was worth less than the money they owed me. I stole for revenge." However, the investigation showed that during the time that she was working as a clerk she was also a prostitute.

The analysis of my material has convinced me that the girls usually did not improve their conditions when they left home. I have had cases where I found that the girl left a comfortable home, and a happy life, and went to a life of depravity, living in a squalid room in want and misery. On questioning, they were unable to give a reason for their action, did not show regret, and admitted, after short questioning, that there really was no palpable reason for their leaving home.

I am aware of the fact that an overwhelming amount of statistical material could be brought against my contention. The main dispute concerns *the importance of the economic status of the delinquent's family as a causative factor in delinquency.* My own cases show that the 498 girls were distributed as to their earnings in the following groups [1] :

1.	Schoolgirls	3
2.	Stenographers	16
3.	Mothers' Helpers	28
4.	Domestics	76
5.	Factory Hands	172
6.	Salesgirls	101
7.	Telephone Operators	21
8.	Office Work	26
9.	Waitresses	18
10.	None	37

The figures show, according to the above classification, that most of them were unskilled workers. As a matter of fact, the earnings of the girls were very much below the amount necessary for maintenance. Out of these 498 girls, 34 gave reliable data as to their earnings, and the earnings of the others, it may be said here, were practically the same.

Up to $10.00 per week	4
From $10.00 to 20.00 per week	18
From $20.00 to 30.00 per week	1
From $30.00 to 40.00 per week	3
Not determined (except domestics)	8

The average earnings were, therefore, about twenty dollars weekly, which, considering that all this money was brought into the house, was not so very bad.

[1] The schoolgirls were high school students. Those claiming no occupation were, as a rule, girls who kept house for their fathers, as the mothers were dead.

The investigation of the family situation showed the following important facts :

(1) The earnings were brought into the house and given to the mother. There were, as a rule, other children working, and all the money formed a pool used towards the maintenance of the house. This was the practice among the foreign born.

(2) The girl was self-supporting, living either with strangers or relatives. In this case she had full control over her earnings.

The families were, as a rule, poor, but very few were in actual want. The immediate cause of delinquency was, with the exception of two cases, never on account of poverty or a desire to better the financial condition.

Moreover, the nature of the offence shows the absence of the economic factor as a cause of delinquency. Only 8 out of 40 girls were arrested for petty larceny (shoplifting), and the articles taken were of no value to the delinquent.

However, if the interpretation of the term " economic status " implies that poverty is a determining factor in the production of the delinquent personality, then I would substitute for this the broader conception of environment, as I showed in the preceding chapter.

On the other hand, we are here concerned not so much with delinquency as a social manifestation, as with the delinquent as a psychological entity. We are concerned, here, with the motives which the delinquent in his simplicity or cleverness gives us as an excuse for his offence, and we are also concerned with the subconscious determining factor which served as the dynamic element.

In dividing the girls into groups, according to the motives which caused their delinquency, we encounter first the great obstacle that it is futile to obtain from them a plausible motive. As far as their mental mechanism is concerned, they were devoid of motives. Their life, during the deciding moments, was in no way different from the daily life that they were leading from their very earliest years. They had grown into and with the misery of family disruption, or, if their family was good, they had always acted in the same abnormal manner. It would, therefore, be futile to attempt to classify motives. We are only able to classify the girls according to the reaction they showed during the examination, when questioned about their offences, and when attempts were made to obtain data concerning their so-called motives. I may remark, here, in passing, that in the entire group (with the negligible exception of about five girls), all accused the parents, but all recanted after a short while, and were very suggestible ; and I found it very easy to make them admit the motives that I wanted them to admit. Their bitterness against the parents ranged from recrimination to real hatred.

It may be interesting to note, here, that delinquency starts early. It is immaterial at what age the actual conflict with the law started. An analysis of the childhood records showed, invariably, that the delinquent was " insubordinate in school ", " a truant ", an " impossible child ", " troublesome to parents ", a " terror to other children ", a " liar ", etc. The delinquent had all or some of these attributes, but in the earlier years there was no motive.

I paid particular attention to the life history of nine girls, all recidivists, and tried to find the motives of their delinquency. The following is their story :

Patient 22 years.   *Motives as given by patient.*

Truancy at 12 years.   Did not like school.
Incorrigible at 15 years.
Wayward at 17 years.
Prostitution at 20 years.   Merry life and easy to be
                                a prostitute.

Patient 17 years.

Correctional Home at 15
  years.
Reformatory at 16 years.   No motive.
Incorrigible at 17 years.

Patient 16 years.

Truancy at 8 years.
Children's Court at 12 years.   No motive.
Stealing at 16 years.

Patient 18 years.

Troublesome in school.
Stealing at 14 years.
Incorrigible at 15 years.   Bad company.
Incorrigible at 16 years.
Prostitute at 17 years.

Patient 16½ years.

School good but slow.
Incorrigible at 15 years.
Incorrigible at 16 years.
Missing at 16 years.   No motive.
Located and placed at work.
Stealing at 16½ years.

Patient 17 years.

Graduated school at 14
  years
Raped and held as witness   Does not care to excuse
  at 15 years.   herself.
Missing at 16 years, but
  located.
Living with a man and
  incorrigible at 17 years.

Patient 16 *years.*	*Motives as given by patient.*
Truancy at 12 years.	Does not like her
Truancy at 13 years.	step-mother.
Incorrigible at 16 years.	

Patient 16 *years.*

Truancy at 12 years.	
Committed to Institution at 13, then placed on probation at 14.	Immoral home.
Prostitution at 15 years.	
Prostitution at 16 years.	

Patient 16 *years.*

Stealing from parents.	
Children's Court at 12 years.	Degeneracy?
Sexual promiscuity at 14 years.	
Prostitution at 16 years.	

In attempting to classify the girls according to the reactions obtained, we have, in the first place, the group giving an average mental quotient. They show psychopathic tendencies. They distinguish themselves by an impudent attitude, by resentment at being brought to an examination, by the sense of superiority they feel over the other girls, by excessive arrogance on account of the legal interference with their plans, and by their bitterness against their parents who came between them and the gratification of their desires. They show, distinctly, paranoid trends; they feel themselves persecuted by the law, by their parents and by all the people who were jealous of their happiness, such happiness consisting in the freedom they attempted to obtain. These girls are more dangerous for the damage they inflict on public health and morals than the feeble-minded. They have a certain amount of intelligence, of native ability; they have learned the intricacies of appealing with tears and sad stories, and they have often convinced a simple-minded magistrate of their innocence. Their career starts with waywardness and ends with their being accessories to serious crimes, to the confidence man, to the gangster and to the drug addict.

In the second class are the feeble-minded, from the low grade defective to the imbecile, and among them we have a very extensive class of unfortunates. They co-operate well and try to help the examiner. They are unable to give any explanation for their acts; they lack abstract concepts, they are frequently amoral, they are easily suggestible, easily led by anybody; they are the tools of the criminal, of the social degenerate and of the disreputable woman.

There is, on the other hand, one group of delinquent girls, where the delinquency is, to all intents and purposes, a psychiatrical problem. In them we see the workings of the subconscious, of a something which is inexplicable to them, but which, on analysis, shows that it is nothing but a refuge from some unpleasant situation. There is no doubt that the delinquency in these girls was a reaction to an unpleasant stimulus, an unconscious opposition to a state of affairs which tended to subdue the ego.

It is impossible, here, to enter into an analysis of these cases, but I will give one illustrative case, which shows what the psychoanalysts call the Oedipus complex, —to my mind, the cause of the delinquency.

N., High school girl, sixteen years old, born in America, of foreign born parents.

Family: Mother died when the patient was six years old. Father is an accountant, a very respectable man of good moral habits. He married, after his first wife's

H

death, and the second wife is a woman of satisfactory reputation. She brought up the two children and took good care of them. One brother is a schoolboy, with a good record. The family surroundings reach a very high standard.

Past : Patient never liked her step-mother. Even as a child she hated her, and could not get her own mother out of her mind. However, she was a good child and made fair progress in school. She graduated from public school at an early age, and went to high school, where she was, at this time, in the third term.

At the age of eleven she was ruined by a man who assaulted her with force. She was ill after that, and she understood what had happened to her. She developed sexually at an early age a few months after the assault. She also developed the habit of stealing money from her parents, which she would use to pay her way to the movies. She had many boy friends, and would stay out with them until late at night, but she never had any sexual relations with them. Her school-work remained good, but her deportment was bad ; she always had trouble with the teachers, was stubborn and spiteful. She was arrogant, disobedient, and impudent in the class-room.

Present : She stole some money from her mother, and when she was discovered she had a quarrel with her parents. She then decided to leave home, and that night (two months ago) she left home. She went to a well-known square in the same city and asked a man if she could be shown to a place where she could get a room. The man took her to a room and told her she could stay with him. She remained with him for a few days and then he told her that he knew a way in which she could make some money. He took her clothes away from her, and gave her different ones and he brought men to her. She gave the money which she earned to the man. He brought so many men to her that she did not see the street for about a week. One day the man brought up two persons with him, and when they came into the room they arrested the entire crowd found there.

Examination : The general physical examination was negative, except for possible pregnancy.

Mental Examination :

> Age : 16 years, 3 months, 16 days
> Terman Score : 14 years, 10 months.
> Intelligence Quotient : .93.

This quotient places the patient at the low end of the average group. She was slightly disturbed and embarrassed by the fact that the examiner knew the entire situation. It was difficult to establish a rapport. The patient worked quickly and logically, co-operating very well and responding to praise in a normal manner. She is able to reason out complex situations into their simpler elements, but has a rather poor score for immediate memory. Her range of tests is limited.

The results of the psychiatrical examination were very interesting in this case. Her step-mother is related to her, but in her child mind she could never reconcile the fact that she came to take her mother's place. She thought that inasmuch as her mother was dead, she herself should really have taken over the duties of the household. For a period of a few years, which elapsed between her mother's death and the remarriage of her father, she felt the heavy responsibilities of a housekeeper, and on many occasions took the part of mother with the other children. The advent of the new mother

meant the usurping of her own rights in the family, and
for this reason she hated the step-mother. Her stealing
was done more to spite the step-mother and, if possible,
to awaken her father against her. She enjoyed seeing
them quarrel. Her behaviour in school and the trouble
she caused everywhere were for the same reason. She
knew that she was considered an unruly girl, but what
angered her most was that she was never able to awaken
sympathy in her father ; she could never make her
father understand her.

Before the assault took place, when she was only
eleven years old, she knew a great deal about sexual
matters, much of it instinctively, and a great deal from
what she overheard people say. She knew about the
birth of children, from what she overheard the pregnant
say, when talking among themselves, or from what
she was told by other children whose mothers expected
to give birth. She knew that the duties of a mother
meant also other things besides keeping house. She
developed quickly after the assault, and did not really
regret the assault, inasmuch as it brought her nearer
to what a mother should be. However, after her father
remarried, her entire personality changed.

This case was very interesting, because it presented
unusual features. We were dealing, here, with a case
of psychoneurosis, and this girl could have been restored
to her proper social surroundings by suitable medical
attention.

There is one common link between these classes
of girls ; they all show over-egotism. The first, with
a polish of pseudo-refinement on top, but with all the
earmarks of degeneracy and intemperance ; the second
group shows an egotism which is primitive, brutal, uncivilized, animal ; on some occasions devoid of cognitive

elements, on others so primitive as to be frightful, and at the same time pitifully simple.

Motives of delinquency in this class of criminals go back to infancy, and can be traced to their shattered childhood, to the absence of proper adjustment, to the defects in our understanding of the biology of social life, of family life, of individual life. It is futile to attempt to find the motives of delinquency in the act or offence of the individual concerned. We must pause and look at the individual as a social unit, as a product of the social organization, as a product not only of the union of two different cells, but also as a product of the environment.

V

ORGANIC INFERIORITY

It was during the world war that observations were first made upon the sudden change in the endocrine functioning of soldiers put under great stress. It was found that many soldiers who possessed gland disturbances, or latent gland dysfunctioning, were prone to suffer from neuroses, attributable to the war. I will mention, here, the frequency of thyroid enlargement in soldiers suffering from so-called shell-shock. It was my experience, while weeding out the various combatants, that soldiers showing any signs of thyroid dysfunctioning were unfit for active combatant service at the front. And yet, these very same young men were leading an active life before entering the service, apparently without any ill effect. Of course, we were unable to measure the emotions of all these combatants —we had neither the means nor the time—but definite information could be obtained.

While approaching the front or under shell fire, the combatant was at ease and discharged his duties properly. It was frequently after he was relieved that a definite syndrome of over-functioning of the thyroid gland was noticed and investigated. Moreover, the soldier admitted that his thyroid was always large. There was no doubt that the emotional strain was responsible for this thyroid disturbance.

In my neuro-psychiatric practice, it has also been my experience that neurotics show definite glandular disturbances. People who suffer from such disturbances are a ready prey to the difficulties in life, are drowned by them and are unable to put up a successful struggle for existence. They show an early discouragement in any struggle, give way to their difficulties and are easily defeated. It is, of course, impossible to say exactly which of the many endocrine glands are the most responsible, but as a rule, we are apparently dealing with a pluriglandular syndrome, in which one gland or another may be the most disturbed. That the endocrines are greatly concerned with our life activities, that they are greatly responsible for our character formation seems beyond doubt, though we are unable to say in just what way they are concerned.

Of course, we could conceive the " character " of an individual as something *per se*, independent of the organic part. In that case, we return to the old-time psychological approach and possibly to metaphysical conceptions and theories. On the other hand, we may find a close relationship between the *organic* and the *psychic*, and trace the development of the psyche from simple reflex actions up to the complicated associations, memory, ideation, etc. We may be able, in such a case, to understand the mechanism of thought, of reasoning, and to grasp, to a great extent, the dynamic power of the higher psychic actions.

As physicians—and not as psychologists—we draw a great proportion of our observations from the study of diseases, or of syndromes, and then from our laboratory work we derive conclusions which help us to interpret the condition. As physicians we also use *common sense* psychology, and we therefore define character as the way in which an individual *behaves* himself in relation to society at large.

We notice, immediately, that behaviour can be conceived only in relation to others, or to some extraneous agent ; in other words, behaviour means a method of reaction.

In our study of disease, we find that a *sick person* behaves himself differently from a well person, and we also find that in certain diseases the entire personality is different and that the character of the individual is different. The bright, alert young man or woman becomes suddenly grouchy, depressed, seclusive. The executive who was a tornado in the office, who preached and showed efficiency, becomes indolent and careless. Another, and of a calm logical mind, becomes temperamental, sensitive, impossible. Moreover, the parents notice that their little girl, who was always obedient, of good deportment in school, and among the first in her class-work, suddenly, at a certain age, becomes sullen, inefficient, impudent, and careless.

In all these persons changes have occurred, without visible signs of disease, changes which make one wonder as to the causes of this inner revolution which has taken place.

It is in such instances that a physical examination, conducted by a competent physician, may reveal that those physical changes were not incidental, but were due to actual organic states of definite organs, the significance of which we are only beginning to grasp, at present.

The incidental discovery made by a physician, that his patient, a girl of eleven, knows more about sex than another girl of fourteen, may lead, on examination, to the fact that he is dealing with a child showing a very

high development of the secondary sexual characteristics. It may also show that the child in question
is a fully developed woman with all the attributes of
womanhood. The seclusiveness, and the abnormal
tendency to introspection shown by that girl may be
explained by the suppression of an early awakening of
the libido with a subsequent development of *habits*.
In such a case, we may deal with a disturbance of the
suprarenal cortex or of the thymus, or a purely ovarian
overfunction which, however, is embryologically derived
from the same layer as the suprarenal cortex. We are
not speaking, here, of çases of precocious puberty which
are pathological, to all intents and purposes, but with
dysfunctioning of the endocrine glands in an otherwise
normal person.

The study of emotional disturbances in adolescents
has led to numerous interesting findings. Watson [1]
mentions the fact that under emotions there is an increase
of the blood-sugar ratio. This is due to the function of
the adrenal glands. In some of my patients I noticed
a great fluctuation in the blood pressure under emotions.

However, the emotionally unstable individual can be
studied under various diseased conditions. The person
suffering from Graves's disease shows a great emotional
strain. These people develop an anxiety neurosis, are
apprehensive and frequently show phobias.

A boy of fifteen was brought to me for an examination,
on the advice of his teacher. Up to the age of fourteen
he was a good scholar. He was rather small for his
age, pale looking and shy. Suddenly, he began to grow,
and during a period of a little over a year he reached
the height of five feet six inches. His hands became

[1] Watson, John B. : *Psychology from the Standpoint of a Behaviorist*, 1919, pp. 189-190.

large and his feet grew greatly. He showed a definite enlarged thyroid gland. He became a truant, and at home he was disobedient and unruly. On closer examination it was found that we were dealing with an endocrinopathy involving the pituitary gland.

We are, at present, able to estimate, more or less correctly, the function of the thyroid gland with the aid of our calculations of the basal metabolic rate. In a series of 15 neurotic women under my care I found that the basal metabolic rate was from $+4$ to -27. The greater number gave a minus figure. In all these patients I was dealing with pre-menopausal conditions.

To ascertain, with a little more precision, the workings of the endocrine system in neurotics, I made the following experiments :

The blood pressure was determined before any history was taken from the patient. Of course, the physician had to be sufficiently well acquainted with the patient to see that she was in a relaxed state. After the reading, the patient was told to repeat the incidents which were held responsible for the onset of the illness. The most striking incidents were brought forward and the patient was requested to visualize these, if possible. Another reading of the blood pressure showed an increase, frequently, of 15 points. The very same results could be obtained if a paragraph from a newspaper or a book describing some sensational occurrence was read to the patient, or if a dream analysis was undertaken. Emotions have, apparently, a great deal to do with the action of the suprarenals.[1]

In matters of growth, we are dealing mostly with the pituitary gland. The pineal gland is also concerned with growth, and both glands are also concerned with

[1] Definite experiments have been described by Cannon.

sex development. We have the opposites in skeletal development, the giant and the dwarf, the exceedingly obese or the very thin individual. Correspondingly, we have, psychically, the dull or backward child, the cretin or the mongol. These, all conditions of a psychic nature, correspond closely with a definite endocrinopathy, and in most of the cases we are dealing with a syndrome, so ably demonstrated by Timme as the pluriglandular syndrome.[1]

The behaviour psychologists attach considerable importance to the adrenals, possibly on account of the work of Cannon. As a physician, I feel myself constrained to remove some of the glory that encompasses the adrenals, and give some of it to other glands that we know more about.

I believe that the thyroid is more concerned with our emotional make-up than any other gland. We have more definite evidence about the thyroid, as we are able to study its manifestations in young children. The cretin is one example of it. Hypothyroid infants show mental defectiveness. Idiocy is a frequent occurrence when the gland is absent. Frequently the gland is present, and the child appears normal to its parents, except for a sullenness and grouchiness which distinguishes it from the other children. When school life starts, a great difficulty is noted. The child does not show results in his work, and the teacher claims that the child, though not definitely backward, is retarded and cannot do the work. An examination will reveal a condition of hypothyroidism. On the other hand, the child may be a hard worker, and with great efforts and good home environment may go through school.

Close observation will reveal that the individual, in

[1] Walter Timme : *Pluriglandular Syndrome.*

spite of his apparent success, is emotionally unstable, fidgety, incapable of decisions at a critical moment. The examination will reveal a hypothyroid state. " A patient of my series," writes Janney, " had suffered from marked symptoms of hypothyroidism since boyhood, weighing at puberty over two hundred pounds and showing marked physical incapacity. His condition remained undiscovered and untreated until middle life. In spite of this, however, this gentleman became prominent in social, civic and literary circles, and was regarded among his friends as a man of unusual mental attainments. Close examination, however, elicited a number of psychic characteristics ascribable to hypothyroidism ; mental instability and restlessness, vacillation and disturbances in the genital sphere. The basal metabolism was minus 30 in the untreated state." [1]

However, in young people where the behaviour is one of striking sullenness, taciturnity, periods of irritability with lack of emotional control, and at the same time mental retardation, or plain dullness, we may suspect —and an examination will reveal—a hypothyroid state, which can frequently be ameliorated by proper therapy.

The counterpart of this condition we may find in states of hyperthyroidism. Here we find a great emotional instability. The patient seems to be in constant fear or, rather, in a fright or terror. The heart beats rapidly, the hands show a fine and rapid tremor, a cold perspiration covers the patient, the voice is tremulous and the eyes have a stary look. Crile made the comparison between the soldier suffering from shell-shock (his physical appearance) and the patient suffering from Graves's disease. These patients have sexual neuroses.[2]

[1] Janney, Nelson, W.: *Hypothyroidism in Endocrinology and Metabolism*, 1922, vol. i, p. 410.
[2] Crile : *The Kinetic Drive.*

The young adolescent girl, who is suffering from a hyperthyroidal condition, no matter how slight and undetected, will show a constant high metabolic rate. Her behaviour will be one of apprehension and suspicion, and she will frequently show sexual habits, increased libido and general instability.

My observations of the delinquents coming under my care gave interesting data. The most frequent finding was an enlarged thyroid, occasionally symmetrically enlarged and often only one side. They did not complain of any symptoms pointing towards its disturbance, but the increase of the thyroid was evident. Occasionally there was a veritable goitre. The mental dullness was probably associated with that, and in such patients we had a late puberty, usually about fifteen or sixteen years of age. These were evident cases of hypothyroidism.

We also found the emotionally very unstable girls, with early sexual offences and early puberty. They showed definite symptoms of hyperthyroidism, in addition to other endocrinopathies. Many times I was inclined to class these among cases of latent Basedow's disease, waiting only for stronger emotional outburst to bring it into prominence. Of course, it was impossible to say just how much the predicament in which the girls found themselves was responsible for it. However, the outstanding point was that, whichever the cause, on account of the generality of the findings among a great majority of the delinquents, we were dealing with a state of this particular gland, making it vulnerable, and showing a congenital physical defect.

The physical appearance of the delinquents was very striking. I found practically two classes, only :

(1) The overgrown girl, well developed, and as a

rule much too old-looking for her age ; the secondary sex characteristics exceedingly well developed, and many of them with absence of womanly grace. Many showed a body formation approaching the male characteristics, the distribution of the hirsutes following the male type, the large feet, the large hands and the formation of the chin. The teeth were found spaced, in a great number, with the characteristic deficiency in calcium.

On questioning, I obtained data which gave further indications of the endocrine dysfunctioning. Irregularities in menstruation, frequent pituitary headache, occasional visual disturbances, chilly sensations of the body, etc.

(2) The second group of girls were those showing a great under-development. Among these we found the moron, the distinctly feeble-minded and the border-line girl. Many girls showed the Mongolian face, the cretinic approachment. They showed distinct thyroid dysfunctioning associated with other glandular disturbances. Inquiries also revealed the fact that they were, most of the time, of an under-developed stature, and did not show any secondary sexual characteristics until late. The menstruation of these girls was, as a rule, scanty, very irregular and painful. In looking over my material, I do not hesitate to say that, with a very small margin, most of them showed distinct endocrine defects which could be traced back to childhood. It was, however, during puberty or, rather, in the immediate post-puberty period that the dysfunctioning had shown itself, and that a distinct type of gland disturbance appeared.

This corresponds exactly with the time that the majority of the girls showed their great change in personality and the beginning of delinquency.

The average age of the onset of menstruation was in most cases between fourteen and sixteen years. Only five showed onset at twelve, and twenty-three at thirteen years. In about 100 girls it could not be determined. However, we can safely say that the onset was at the age mentioned. The incidence of delinquency in the 498 girls showed :

First offence at	11 years or before		12 girls
,, ,, ,, 12	,,	,,	6 ,,
,, ,, ,, 14	,,	,,	9 ,,
,, ,, ,, 16	,,	,,	241 ,,
,, ,, ,, 17	,,	,,	170 ,,
,, ,, ,, 18	,,	or above	60 ,,

Out of this number, a total of 325 girls gave information (examination by a physician) as to the incidence of sexual relations, and 237 have had sexual relations ; 11 of these 237 before the age of fourteen years.

It would be erroneous to attribute the delinquency to gland disturbances, but we are able to draw a parallel conclusion with that found in neurotics. The presence of such a disturbance shows nothing but the vulnerability of certain individuals, an emotional state which is not like the normal, and manifestations of that emotional state in various forms, from neurosis to delinquency, depending upon causes extraneous to the individual himself.

In the general psychic make-up we find a remarkable kinship between the neurotic and the delinquent. Apart from the hereditary and environmental factors, we also find a great deal of similarity in the endocrine status.[1] The neurotic, as well as the delinquent, shows mentally only two types, the dull and the over-alert,

[1] By a "neurotic" we understand, here, the condition classed medically as a psychoneurosis, which is very different from the lay conception.

but both categories show a high degree of emotional instability. From clinical observations upon both I draw the conclusion that this emotional instability is a direct result of an endocrinopathy. There must have been, from the very start in life, a *locus minoris resistentiæ* in the endocrine system, making these individuals vulnerable under the exigencies of life.

What we call emotional instability is, on closer analysis, *emotional defectiveness*, and the endocrine deficiency represents, in ultimate analysis, an actual *organic inferiority*.

In this sense we notice a glimmer of truth in the old Lombrosian theory of the born criminal. The frequent physical defects that we find in criminals (habitual) have their explanation in the involvement of the endocrine glands concerned with growth and life activities. The conception of the born criminal, in the Lombrosian sense, was the result of the inadequacy of the medical knowledge of that time. However, if in the place of the born criminal we put forward the conception of the *constitutional inferior* we approach an understanding of a true condition of facts.

The delinquent—who is on closer observation a criminal in the making—is to all intents and purposes, medically, a quite definite constitutional inferior. The conception of constitutional inferiority is not a medical term of a vague meaning, covering our ignorance, but a true state of emotional defectiveness, as a result of an actual organic inferiority transmitted by heredity.

This constitutional inferiority is the fundament from which delinquency may grow out, as a defective attribute of a defective emotional make-up. Delinquency is not inborn, but is a product of environmental factors upon a faulty constitution.

The frequency of mental retardation among delinquents (the term mental retardation meaning an intelligence quotient below .90) indicates the rate of involvement of the endocrine system. This involvement has, no doubt, been present since birth, as the school reports point out that the children were retarded. Also, the fact that out of the 498 girls only 78 were grammar school graduates, and that most of the others never got beyond 6B, also showed the sluggishness of their mentality. I may also add that with very, very few exceptions all the girls left school at the age of fifteen, showing that even those who were permitted to be promoted were at least two years retarded in their school work.

Coupled with this fact of mental retardation, we also have the fact that in a number of instances other children in the same family were rarely on the same level with the delinquents. This would show that though the other children were brought up under the same circumstances, they possessed something which permitted their complete adjustment to the environment, whereas the delinquents were vulnerable.

I may also mention, here, a fact pointed out in a previous chapter, that many delinquents were removed from their parents, and were brought up under very favourable conditions. Under the strain of great emotional stress, however, they became delinquents.

All this points to the fact that all these girls were constitutional inferiors in the sense discussed above. Delinquency as a behaviour reaction is only an incident in the life of such an individual.

I

VI

EMOTIONS *vs.* INTELLIGENCE [1]

There is no doubt that an analysis of the material which I am giving here will show that the mental status of the patient is not sufficient to explain the delinquency. There is no doubt that the mental defect shown by some delinquents may explain the rôle of the intellect in the production of delinquency, but the fact that two individuals of a different mental status may commit the same offence shows that other, more potent, causes are at the bottom of the condition.

Moreover, there are numerous mental defectives who have no doubt grown up under similar circumstances and have not become delinquents, and there are numerous individuals who are not defectives, yet are delinquents.

The analysis of the material shows, primarily, that the deciding moment of the action was, as a rule, impulsive. It took one moment's action to determine the leaving home, the stealing of an article from a store, or going with a young man into a room. A well-laid plan never existed. Matters were not talked over with anybody, and, as a matter of fact, the girl never thought of it before. That is, as a rule, ascribed to the easy suggestibility of the girl. We read in many of the reports that she was easily led, was easily suggestible, and

[1] The author does not intend to discuss here the psychology of emotions. He happens to be a great admirer of Höffding, and he could not avoid looking at the problem from such an angle. However, the subject of this chapter is an analysis of the delinquents, and not a psychological controversy.

had no power of discrimination. In saying that, we are confused between what belongs to feeling and what belongs to intellect. Now, it is true that in a decided mental defective there is not much power of discrimination, but in many dullards there is such a power, and that is exactly the reason why they are held legally responsible. However, what is forgotten is that the entire action was done under the power of emotions, and that during the deciding moment the intellect played no rôle whatsoever.

I ascribe to the emotions a greater rôle than to the mental status as a causative agent in delinquency.

The mental defective approaches emotionally not the child so much as the primitive. His emotions are few in number, but they pass easily into passion. In the civilized and adult individual the emotions are numerous, are not so strong and do not pass easily into passions. If we take the example of anger, which is an emotion, in the defective it passes easily into revenge, whereas in the normal individual it will subside and rarely pass into the passion of revenge. I will call attention, here, to two of my patients, who were arrested for shoplifting. They went to the store without thought of stealing. Both of them had an unpleasant occurrence. One worked in the store and was refused her salary because she asked for more than she was entitled to. She became very angry, and when she went into the store, she took a dress from the counter, because of the injustice done to her. The second one also went to the store, where she had worked for one week. After she had received her salary, someone stole her pocket-book, and she stole some stockings from the store to repay an injustice done to her.

The intellectual process in these two cases could

be analysed, but it would not lead to any conclusions, as the girls related that before they went into the store they never thought of stealing. It was only when they were in the store and saw things they liked that they remembered that someone stole their money, and they therefore took the things. Of course, they always wished for such articles as the ones that they stole. It evoked great pleasure to look at these things, even if some were of no use to them.

One of the girls was classed, after a mental test, as of average intelligence, and the conversation that I had with her was interesting. There were two things outstanding in this girl's mind. Firstly, that after she had worked an entire week someone stole her bag, and secondly, that her bag was stolen while she was in the store. The day she stole the articles she had visited two other department stores, looked at and handled various articles exhibited on the counter, and at no time did she think of appropriating any of those articles. It was only while visiting the store where she had lost her bag that the thought of stealing came into her mind, and she committed the act.

Let us examine the cases arrested for incorrigibility and waywardness :

In this class we are dealing with girls giving an I.Q. of the average normal, border-line or dullard. In one or two instances we also have morons. There are two very important factors in the life of the girl to decide the offence. In the first place, there is the " quarrel " at home. As a rule it is preceded by the girl either staying out late at night, or some other disobedience to the guardians' orders. The second factor is a sudden and not premeditated action of the girl—the act of leaving home. Plans were not made, the moment chosen for leaving home was, most of the time, inopportune, for it came so unexpectedly. However, we see first the appearance of anger. The cause of this appearance is undoubtedly the fact that the guardian attempted to curb the ego, to deny the girl the pleasure " she experienced in staying out late ".

For example, the following is part of a conversation between myself and a delinquent during the examination :

" What made you leave home ? "

" I don't know, but I was very angry at the time."

" Why were you angry ? "

" Mother scolded me. I was out late that night, and when I came home she called me names and told me I was a bad girl."

" Was that the first time she had scolded you ? "

" No, she has done that many times, but just that night I had such a good time, and I met some nice young men." Then she added, " I know how to take care of myself."

In this last assertion we could see the trend of thought of the girl. However, the following is what happened :

" Did you know where to go ? "

" No, I just left the house and went out into the street. I had no money with me. I never thought that I might need some money. I was very, very angry, I could have done anything at that time, and I hated my mother. Then I met the young man who had been arrested. He spoke to me, and told me to go with him, and I went."

" But you said before that you knew how to take care of yourself, yet you did not act so."

" The only thing I know is that I was very angry, and did not care. He was a nice man, and I forgot about the scolding, and went with him."

There is no doubt that analysts would call the trend of thought of this girl the yearning for freedom. As a matter of fact, it is the result of the overstrong ego, the egotism which was the force here. We see here again the passing over of the emotion of anger into the passion of revenge, to get even with a mother who dared interfere with the aim of pleasure. The intellect has played absolutely no part in it at all. The girl left her home without even taking sufficient money for a meal, and took no clothing. The man who took her to a room was unknown to her; he was a man she had met for the first time, and he came in the rôle of protector. The instinct of self-preservation came again into play, and the girl went with him. Though she " knew how to take care of herself," the intellect was blank at that time, and she went.

There is no great difference between this group of girls and the other group. The basis of their action is the ego, and the interference with the aims of the ego brings forth the action. We analyse the girls during their childhood and recognize two groups :

In the first group, we have the girls who had a good record as children. Their parents or their guardians will say that they never gave any trouble during childhood. However, close questioning reveals the following facts : That they were considered different from the other children in the household ; that they were stubborn when interfered with. They were peculiar in many ways. They were headstrong. As a rule, they were docile and obedient, but occasionally they would be troublesome. The other children, like all children, would occasionally have the same outburst, but the difference was that the outburst of the subsequent delinquent was strong and destructive. I would call attention to one case where the father and mother both admitted that the girl was a good child, but she had to be petted and she had to be indulged in. In another case the remark was made that she was a nervous child, and had a temper. It can be seen that in a household, let us say, of four children, the parents noticed that there was a difference between the children. They suffered from emotional outbursts far stronger than the usual normal child suffers.

These emotional outbursts came often, whenever an interference took place. But at other times the child was docile and full of joy. Now, in matters of joy we also have information of interest. " She was a happy child when she had her way." This statement is important if brought into relation with the statement " that happiness was extreme, that even the joy was of the same unbounded and destructive kind ". She could break things for joy ; she could do anything for joy. It was another manifestation of an overstrong egotism : but the chief peculiarity of these children was the ease with which they passed from one emotional state into another. At one moment she was destructively angry and the next moment (when she was given what she wanted) was destructively joyful. There is no doubt that there was excessive emotional instability. No doubt, too, in observing normal children, we notice this emotional instability. But in the normal case, neither anger nor joy is of sufficient strength to frighten the parents and make them feel just as much worried at one thing as at the other.

In the second group we have those girls who had a bad record as children. From early childhood they showed the difference between themselves and the others. They were exceedingly egotistic, quarrelled with the other children in the house, broke things and beat their playmates. These children played by themselves, were seclusive, except, for example, when they saw another child holding a toy, which they would immediately snatch. When they became a little older they stole things, especially food from the house, sweets and money. They did not confide in other children; they were by themselves. They did not show love or even affection, but were always trying to get what they saw and liked. They were gourmands. They lied with or without cause. Love and affection did not make them happy or joyful, but when they obtained the thing they were after they were full of delight and secluded themselves to enjoy what they had obtained. In school, they were always in trouble and made trouble for the teachers. They tattled on the other children, they got other children into trouble and invented stories about the teachers. They appeared as witnesses against the teacher and accused him of immorality and perversities. They stole whenever and whatever they could.

Everywhere we find written the ego of these children. Irrespective of their mental status they were egotists, destructively so, and harmful to their surroundings. With them, if it were possible to measure the emotions we would find that the emotion of anger lasted but an instant and immediately became the passion of revenge. The latter lasted longer and increased in intensity until it became destructive. These children practically did not know emotions. Such as they had were simple and of short duration, changing rapidly into passions.

The following history of Rose H., a girl of fifteen, who caused great suffering to a fifty-six year old teacher, is instructive, and demonstrates the points mentioned.

Rose was a former patient of the clinic, where she was treated for repeated attacks of chorea. My first acquaintance with her was when she started going to school, at the age of seven years. She was the youngest child of the family, and she was what her mother termed " very spoiled ". Her school record was not very good. Her attendance was bad, first on account of illness, and secondly because she disliked school. She was very stubborn at home, and fabricated a good deal. Frequently she caused trouble between her sister, or a neighbour and her mother. However, the first indication of her true personality was when, on my suggestion, she was sent to a convalescent home. She was sent home within two weeks, with the following notations : " Quarrelsome ", " liar ", " bad habits " (masturbation), and " unmanageable ". She was then thirteen years old. However, she was greatly improved and was sent back to school. About two weeks after she brought her mother to school to complain against her teacher, who did not treat her right, who was discriminating against her and punishing her. With the advice of the hospital social worker, she was put into another class, with another teacher of the same faith as hers, and known for her tact in handling children. Towards the end of the term we intervened again ; this time it appeared that the teacher was accusing her of having stolen some change from her desk. We succeeded in having her transferred to another school, where the principal himself was of the same faith.

For an entire year we had lost track of her, but the following year the visiting teacher notified me that Rose had brought charges against a man teacher, fifty-six years old, of an unquestionable reputation. The charges were :

(1) Unbecoming conduct—consisting in petting her in the class-room.

(2) Impairing morals—by sitting her on his lap and feeling her body.

Moreover, Rose was not satisfied with that only, but also mentioned the names of other schoolmates who had the same grievances.

The mental test showed average intelligence.

The investigation of the case showed the following :

Rose's school record was bad, and she made up her mind that she did not want to continue going to school. She had quarrelled, that day, with one of her class-mates, who was one of the best scholars, and the teacher called her attention to the fact that the other child was brighter and that he liked her better.

That evening she told her mother that there was a scandal in school, and told of a " love affair " between the teacher and the other pupil. Suddenly she screamed : "And he also did not conduct himself properly with me ".

Of course the investigation exonerated the teacher, and Rose was put into another class.

We notice, in this case, the sudden outburst of the accusation, unpremeditated, brought forward by hatred. It is unquestionable that her accusation was unthought of one second before it was made. A typical case of passion as a dynamic force of her action.

In the case of emotions, we are not dealing with cognitive elements. To be under the power of emotion means that the person in question has no cognition of the fact. Emotions are derivatives of feelings, and they are a sudden outburst of feeling. The individual concerned has no time to have the elements of cognition brought into play. They are entirely outside the control of the individual. The feeling upon which he proceeds is the feeling of pain or pleasure, and it is based upon the psychological process of repetition. The first element was a feeling of pain and the development of dislike or aversion. A repetition of the same experience will bring forth, in the course of time, the emotion of dislike, aversion. The individual does not have to pass through the experience and have the feeling of pain. The occurrence in itself will awaken in him the emotion of dislike, aversion, anger, without the cognitive elements associated originally with the awakening of the feeling of pain, However, a repetition of the emotion will weaken it, and in the course of time it will not awaken any more emotions. For example, a landscape seen for the first time will delight us, and will awaken in us the emotion of reverence, but if that same landscape is seen frequently, it will cease to awaken any emotion in us.

Passion, on the other hand, is the kinetic form of emotion. It is action, and by repetition it increases in strength. It is also devoid of cognitive elements, and it is rightly said that a man commits a murder in a fit of passion ; he did not know what he was doing.

To say, therefore, that emotions were the motive power behind his delinquency means that the cognitive element was missing ; that the individual in question did not reflect and acted without thought. Emotions are the sparks which inflame and give rise to the real force—passion.

It was said above that emotions disappear through repetition, whereas passion increases in intensity. That may cause a confusion if not analysed carefully. If the presence of a certain food produces the emotion of dislike, it will unquestionably produce the same emotion each time the food is put before us, on the table, and that could be an argument against this. However, if looked into carefully, it will be seen that though the first time or times it was certainly an emotion of aversion that was awakened, after a while that emotion will not be awakened, but in its place will arise the passion of hatred. It will frequently be accompanied by the action of destroying the food and thereby removing the cause of the trouble. The linking chain, therefore, between the causative factor and the appearance of passion does not necessarily have to come into existence. A number of inter-associating elements may be missing, except the first and the last element, the original cause and the ultimate effect.

The history of two cases is instructive in that respect, and will illustrate the truth of the opinion expressed above.

S. was a girl of seventeen when brought to court as incorrigible. Her father made the complaint against her, and among the accusations were the following important facts : She did not work, stayed out late at night, kept company with notorious gangsters in the neighbourhood, beat her mother, and was an all around nuisance.

It was not the first time that the girl was before the Court. As a school child, beginning with the age of eleven, she was troublesome in the class. She was mentally somewhat retarded, but she would have been able to do better work if only her conduct had been better. She played truant in school, insulted the teachers, stole small articles in the class, and was continuously quarrelling with the other pupils. She left school at the age of fourteen, and went to work. She never kept a position for any length of time. She liked the places where she could associate with bad boys, and she was soon ruined by a man whose name she did not know.

She lived with that man for a while, until her father took her home, and she again went to work.

This is, in short, the history. However, what is missing, here, is the fact that her own mother died when she was eleven years old, and that five months after her mother's death her father re-married.

Investigation showed that until the age of eleven, that is, until her mother's death she was a good child and never gave any trouble, but that after her father re-married she began to behave badly. It can be stated that her misbehaviour started at the age of eleven, from the time that her father re-married. It was a change similar to that which we have often seen in delinquents, coming on with the onset of menstruation, when a complete psychic change takes place. It was impossible to show that prior to that time there was any complaint against the girl. She was a docile child, not very bright, but very quiet in school and able to do her work with a certain amount of satisfaction.

During the period of five months, from the time of her mother's death until her father's re-marriage, she took her duties seriously. She had a vague sensation that she was the mother of the family, that she must take care of her little brother, and that she must keep house. Of course, she was unable to fulfil the duties of a mother, but that was her feeling, and in her games with the other children she imagined herself the mother of her little brother, and conducted herself like her mother did when she was alive.

Without any previous knowledge, her dreams were shattered when her father brought home his second wife. She never became used to calling her mother, but called her " aunt ", and she hated her from the first day on. In the first place, she considered the second wife as an intruder, for she took her mother's place; and secondly, she destroyed her own prominence in the family life. After her mother's death she had assumed prerogatives in the home ; now she was robbed of the importance of a mother, and all her dreams were shattered. She hated her step-mother to such an extent that she would have done anything to make her feel badly. She especially wanted to play upon her father's sympathy She knew that her father would sympathize with her in case of a quarrel, and she began to tell tales about her step-mother—that she was not economical and that she was mistreating her. However, this plan did not turn out as she had expected ; her father punished her on the slightest complaint. She then began to make her step-mother miserable in other ways. Her behaviour in school was bad ; her step-mother was frequently called to school, and the girl began to play truant. She thought her father would accuse the step-mother of not taking care of her. She remembers the day when she was brought to the Children's Court as a truant from school. She was happy that she was in the limelight, that somebody else might listen to her story about her step-mother and her troubles at home. But instead of that, the judge asked her no questions, but merely told her that she must go to school.

S. did not improve. She went from bad to worse, and was brought again to Court, this time under the charge of incorrigibility, and she was again put on probation. The probation officer reported that she never behaved herself, that she always made trouble for the mother, and that she hated the mother to the utmost. When she was again brought before the judge as an incorrigible, she was sent to a reformatory.[1]

[1] The actual charge was prostitution, but it could not be sustained

In this case we see the passion with which this girl hated her mother. We cannot speak about it as an emotion, for it was more than that. It was passion, and with it we find associated the most destructive of all passions, the passion of revenge. After all, in analysing the case, we see at the bottom of it nothing else but the instinct of self-preservation, the desire to have the most out of life in a childish way.

The mental test of this girl gave her an I.Q. which placed her among the dullards, and according to the examination she was entirely aware of what is right and what is wrong, yet she acted entirely against her knowledge. An analysis suggested that this was one of the cases where proper treatment would have brought a cure for her conduct, that it was a question of a misunderstanding of her situation, and that she would have become a useful girl if she had been handled properly at the proper time. Moreover, the analysis showed that her mentality played no rôle whatsoever in the delinquency, that it was a case of emotionality, primarily, and of the transformation of the emotionality into passion. The lowered mental age showed its lack of power in the fact that it played no rôle, that it had no control over her feelings.[1]

A similar case, with some variations, is the case of N.

N., shopgirl, seventeen years old, foreign born, of foreign-born parents.

Family : Her mother died six years ago, and her father re-married five months after. Her father is a furrier, works steadily and supports the family. She has one sister, who is a schoolgirl and has a good record. There are three other children in the house, but they

---

[1] The " father fixation " in this case is very interesting. It was a typical case for psychoanalysis, but, unfortunately, this was not possible.

are step-brothers, and one step-sister. They are all of good character. Her step-mother is crippled with rheumatism, but is a woman of good character and good reputation. The girl, however, states that her step-mother has a bad temper, and that she abuses her frequently.

Past : When her own mother died she was only eleven years old, and it was very difficult for her to take care of herself and her sister. Her father went to work, and the two children were left in the care of neighbours. At that time her school-work was neglected, and after her father re-married she began to play truant from school. She was then brought before the Children's Court and placed on probation. However, she was not a good girl in school and disliked school-work as well as her step-mother. At the age of fifteen she left school to go to work, and her first job was in a candy factory, where she packed candy. She never kept a position for any length of time. She never worked steadily, and she always returned to the same place for work. For the past year she had been causing trouble to her parents. She remained out very late at night, went to dances with boys who had a bad reputation, and roamed around the streets. She abused her parents and did not get along well with the people in the house. She was unclean in her person and used very bad language to the children.

Present : A few days ago her father objected to her working in the place where she was employed, because he found out that she kept bad company. It came to a quarrel between herself and her step-mother. The next day, when her mother asked her to go for a doctor for her own brother, who was taken ill, she refused, and began to abuse her. She then kicked and beat her mother, who, being a cripple, could not defend herself.

Her father had her arrested, and she was brought before the Court as an incorrigible.

The history, as obtained, needed changes after the girl was questioned closely, and an attempt at analysis was undertaken. It appears that the description of the girl as it was given was correct. It also appears that the step-mother was not very kind to the girl, but the condition could not be changed, as the girl hated her step-mother and stated this whenever she could. It is to be noted that the sudden change which took place occurred soon after her father re-married, when she ceased to be a good and obedient child, began playing truant and had acquired a bad temper.

When the girl was narrating her story she contradicted herself continuously, and when she was told that she was doing so, she admitted that she was telling an untruth. She admitted that she told lies often, and also admitted that she lied many times to get her step-mother angry, " to get her goat ".

She resented her father's re-marriage as soon as it happened, because he " should have known that he could never replace my mother ". She had no other objection to her step-mother. She stated that she was a good woman and brought her up nicely, that she tried many times to please her. She worked for her, kept her clean and mended her clothes. " But she never kissed me, and never took me in her lap, when I was a little girl." The girl stated that it was not sufficient that she had a bed to sleep in and food to eat. She wanted her step-mother to love her, and she did not.

There is no doubt that the instinct of self-preservation is the most conservative element in our psychical make-up. As such, it is transmitted by heredity, and it is common to all living organisms, irrespective of the scale.

K

The intellect has no power over it, for it acts without judgment and without reason. It appears during life as a method of reaction to painful stimuli, and we observe it as such. The feeling of pain or pleasure is the signal for its manifestation. Emotions develop, and are often instantaneous whenever something obnoxious comes into contact with us, or when something pleasurable comes into our presence. The outburst of feeling is seen in the form of emotions, our emotions are impulsive and we act accordingly. Our actions are then impulsive. This is more true of primitive races, of the uncivilized nations, and of certain kinds of people. This is also the characteristic of the delinquents. Their actions are mostly impulsive ; they never lay any plans or formulate a method of action and never talk things over. Possibly, if other circumstances could have prevailed at the critical moment, they would have performed a deed of heroism instead of a crime. When we speak of a man having an uncontrollable temper, it really means that under certain circumstances his emotions suffer a sudden outbreak and he acts entirely on impulse. We may just as well say that " his emotions got the better of him ". When we say that such a man should have thought first before acting, we proclaim a psychological impossibility, for his intellect had absolutely no controlling power, and that is exactly what was wrong with that man ; he was a man acting in an impulsive manner. He suffered from emotional instability. Emotionally, he approached the primitive races ; he is emotionally a backstroke in the scale of human evolution.

However, the intellect has, undoubtedly, some rôle in the development of emotionality, and that is another very important point. But before passing on to that point, it is well to give the history of a case, showing the complete absence of plan formulation in the delinquent, and how impulsiveness is the factor causing emotional individuals to sway their actions one way or another.

R. was a girl of seventeen, born in this country of American parents. Her father was a labourer, but was not able to work, on account of a chronic pulmonary disease. Her mother was forced to support the home by working in a nearby factory. The child-life of the girl was a life of want and misery. She had two sisters, of whom she had to take care during the day, when her mother was working. Occasionally, when his health permitted, her father would also work, and then there would be more food in the house. R. was the oldest in the family, and she soon realized that she would have to work in order to help in the house. This rôle quite pleased her, because she liked to stay at home and take care of the house. She hated school, was slow in her work, never made any progress and had to repeat classes. She also played truant occasionally, at this time staying at home and helping in the house. She soon learned to tell lies for the purpose of staying at home. She would tell her teacher that she was ill or that her mother needed her. However, she was never brought before a Children's Court. When she ceased going to school she was in the 6th Grade. Her home life, during all that time, was a life of drudgery, but she never resented it, because her mother let her alone. When she left school and started to go to work, her mother would admonish her, telling her that she must be in the house at an early hour, and that she must never stay out with the boys in the street. She turned in all the money she earned to her mother, and was given enough for her daily expenses. She never had any amusements, never went anywhere, and the first time she went to a moving picture theatre was when a young man, whom she had met casually, invited her to go. That night she came home late, and her mother scolded her. She went out of the house and met a young man to whom she told her story. He took her to his room, where he ruined her. She did not return home, but remained with him. The next day she came home, and told her mother that she was staying with friends, and returned to the young man until she was arrested.

Here is the short history of a girl who, apparently without any reason, goes into the street, as we would say, to " cool herself off ", and meets a young man whom she does not know, to whom she tells her story about the scolding she has received, and without any inquiry goes with him and lives with him. The only thing she knew about this young man was that his name was " Joe ". After her arrest, she never saw him. However, she was left pregnant and diseased.

What was the primordial motive of her action ? It certainly was not the scolding, for it was not the first time that she received a scolding, and, moreover, at other times she had received more severe punishment from her mother. Then, also, she did not go out of the house for the purpose of leaving ; she went outside to stay for a while. In analysing, we see it was the emotionality of the patient caused by a revolting ego against infringement of the instinct of self-preservation, the avoidance of the curtailment of personal liberty as conceived, or rather felt, by a primitive ego. It was a question of avoidance of pain and the seeking of pleasure. The girl was primitive emotionally, and her actions were determined by a sudden emotional outburst when the young man offered her the only thing that these types are looking for, sympathy, and pleasure given by this sympathy. The action of this girl was impulsive, instantaneous, and the first word of the young man won his point. It was not a question of deciding, as there was nothing to decide ; it was a question of showing the ego a way out of the difficulty.

Moreover, R. could have done differently. She could have done what J. did. The first circumstances in the life of J. are similar to those of R., with the exception that the former's father was dead, and that her mother was working hard to make ends meet. The first experience of J. was when her mother was very much upset about the talk in the neighbourhood that J. was a bad girl and that she kept bad company. Once or twice her mother remonstrated and threatened to have her arrested. However, J. was working more or less steadily, and the mother needed her money. One night she came home late, and her mother told her that she would have to cease doing that, and that she would have to be home at ten, at the latest. The following evening she went to a dance and remained there until midnight. After that time she was afraid to go home, and went with the young man to his house. She was ruined by him, and he then sent her to a friend of his, who lived with her for a little over a week, until she was arrested. But J. was not arrested as an incorrigible, for the day of her arrest she went to work, as she had done every day, and gave her earnings to the man with whom she had been living. What she did, was to steal the money from the drawer in the place where she was working, because the young man with whom she was living told her the way to get easy money. She gave it to him, and never saw him afterwards. The only thing she knew about the man was that his name was Frank. She never inquired, and was never anxious to know a thing about him, for she never thought about it.

These two cases are representative cases, showing an impulsive form of behaviour, when emotions are all too strong, and are the only power behind our actions. It also shows the absence of the intellectual controlling power, the absence of any reason, thinking or judgment.

However, it may be argued that by having a sensation of pain or pleasure a cognitive element is included, that one is aware of the pain or pleasure. That is no doubt so at the beginning of an experience upon which, evolutionally, the feelings and then the emotions are developed. Later in life the intermediary associative elements are lost, and all that appears are the effects. Moreover, it is not necessary to give, here, the psychological theories of feeling and cognition, but only in a general way the important points which will demonstrate our subject ; nor do we intend to enlarge upon the concrete and abstract sensations, or upon the various conceptions appertaining thereto.

As stated above, we cannot easily admit that an individual acts as an automaton, that there is absolutely no judgment in the action. It would mean that the actions were instinctive and reflex. As a matter of fact they are not. When the girl, after a scolding, leaves home and meets the young man in the street and agrees to go where he wants her to go and live with him, then steals the money from her employer because he told her to do so, we cannot say that all these actions of the girl were reflex acts, without the girl knowing what it was all about.

Admitting that she was well aware what she was doing, how can we say that the actions were done under the power of emotions ? And how can we claim that the girl in question was not responsible and that judgment was not a part of her actions?

In analysing the case histories, we draw the important conclusion that the first acts were entirely emotional, that is, in the sense that the discriminating power of the intellect was not there. If a normal individual, intellectually and emotionally, were told that passing a certain street during the night he incurs the danger of being killed, and if he had the choice between two streets to reach a certain point, he would undoubtedly avoid the dangerous thoroughfare. His intelligence would discriminate between the two streets. He would choose, and the choice would not take more than a second, although he may not even show the fact that he chooses. He would not necessarily have to stop and put the problem in his mind and say, " That street is dangerous, I will not pass there." He would turn around and choose another street. In the same way, if a person, intellectually and emotionally normal, suddenly, in the middle of the street, while passing a certain thoroughfare, heard revolver shots, he would suddenly turn and run for cover. He would not stop to judge and say to himself that he may be in danger, but he would act.

We do not expect the girl—when approached by a young man, asking her to go with him up into his room —to stop and say, " I don't know this man ; he is a stranger and means no well ; it is dangerous to go with him." Such a mental process never takes place. But through life we have been evolving a simplified process which never takes place consciously, but which determines our decision, a decision which has the appearance of being an instinctive act.

We notice, in all our cases, that all the answers to

the stimuli received were in a direct line with the stimuli, never in opposition :

"Will you go up into my room ? " " Yes."

"Open the drawer and take the money." "Yes."

It is a simple mental process always in the direction suggested. This shows absence of discrimination.

We also notice that the dynamic force directing the action follows the same line :

Infringement of ego at home (nagging, scolding, threats) $\longrightarrow$ pain as a result $\longrightarrow$ to accept the invitation $\longrightarrow$ freedom from nagging, scolding, threats—pleasure.

But the mechanism is simple only when the first and the last part of the process takes place and the girl follows the simplest suggestion directed only by feeling towards pleasure.

However, we must make here a sharp demarcation between the delinquent (who, as I pointed out above, should be conceived as a criminal in the making) and the actual criminal. We may draw a parallel with the neurotic, whom medically we may term the hysteric, and the initial attack of the neurosis. The first attack is an emotional outburst, also devoid of cognitive elements, but later a " reasoning out " of the condition takes place, with a subsequent fixation of the neurosis.

That fixation may also be observed in neurotics suffering from habit spasms. A soldier, while on the front during the Great War, was exposed to shell fire. One shell burst in front of him, burying in mud and dirt a number of men. He was not hurt, but the following day he complained that he had a pain in his right shoulder, which made him involuntarily move his right arm up and down. The movements were like those made by a man who would attempt to ward off a blow. A few weeks later he was evacuated to a Base Hospital, suffering from " shell-shock " manifested in constant rapid blinking of his eyes, and coarse, defensive movements of his right arm.

We had, here, a fixation of a movement which, at this time, could be rightly called a neurosis.

Delinquency is entirely an emotional outburst, but if no treatment takes place we obtain a fixation of this mental state into the actual state of criminality. One is a condition amenable to treatment, but not the other.

I endeavoured, in the foregoing pages, to look at the subject from a medical standpoint and to analyse the question in the same way as a medical question would be analysed. Irrespective of the mental defectiveness of the delinquent, I believe that the prime and fundamental reasons for delinquency lie in other places than the mental defect. I attribute more importance to the emotional defect. However, emotional defectiveness is not a product of environment, but is an inherent state in a certain individual. It is a congenital defect.

This group of individuals forms what we may rightly call constitutional inferiors. The rôle of environment, shown in the preceding pages, is one of moulding, of bringing about an equilibrium, an adjustment. It is taken as proved that an individual with a normal emotional make-up is born with the potentiality for that adjustment. There is no doubt that such an individual, if put in an environment which I described as not in disequilibrium, will also develop a maladjusted personality. I considered, in another place, such personalities, and I showed that they form the bulk of our psychoneurotics. On the other hand, it is the emotionally inferior who constitute the chief class of delinquents, and who practically form the bulk of them and give rise to the problem of delinquency.

In the study of all the delinquents who came under my observation, I found that I had to deal not only with delinquency as such, but also with families who could not possibly have given us a different kind of an individual. The few exceptions that I met were direct results of an improper training, and a disregard of the essentials in child psychology. On the other hand, in such cases also we were concerned with the problem which confronts us, particularly in this country, of a family who could not harmonize with a social organization so much at variance with their own.

CONCLUSIONS

The delinquents studied in the preceding pages are representative of many thousands of similar cases. The story may vary, from girl to girl, but through all of them runs a thread which shows their close relationship.

A striking point was that forty-eight per cent. were children of foreign-born parents, and only a small number of the girls (29) were themselves foreign born.

As will be noticed from the study of the cases, the question of heredity, or transmission of taints from the parents, is not tenable in all of them. The parents of many girls were, more or less, respectable and honourable people. This held true, especially, for girls accused of waywardness. In two or three of the cases the parents and other members of the family were, indeed, people of some standing. The reason for the delinquency, therefore, must be looked for in another direction.

The delinquents could be divided, from the psychological standpoint, into two groups :

(1) The girls—usually wayward minors—in whom a plausible excuse for their delinquency was not apparent. However, if we remove from this list about eight delinquents, we have the rest who were classified, on the psychometric test, as dullards, low average, or border-line.

Two of the girls had graduated at an early age, making exceedingly good progress, but in spite of this fact they were dullards. It appears that during their school life they were what we might call " hard workers ", girls who rarely played, rarely had any other amusements, but who passed their spare time in doing their school-work. That is a condition which corresponds, exactly, with the parents' conception of a " good child ". What intelligence could not accomplish in those children, hard work in school did accomplish, and they were, in fact, pushed forward from class to class as long as their school-work was satisfactory.

There is a possibility that some of them showed a gradual going back in their mental aptitude. This is a fact well known in medicine. In the first place, the existence of various infectious diseases in childhood may have been responsible for an arrest in the mental development in childhood, and secondly, the condition of slight mental backwardness may have existed from birth, but so slight that up to a certain age it could not be detected. Only later, when the basal age was reached, could that mental backwardness be seen, and it showed the exact condition of the girl.

As can be seen from the study of the cases in this group (83 in all), they all showed a great docility of character during childhood. Their parents attested that during childhood they gave no trouble and were obedient. However, they were always markedly selfish and showed some temper. This outburst would come at certain times, but then it would be quite marked. Their so-called docility was expressed by the fact that one could do what he wanted with them. However, the child could not be crossed, and " when she was good, she was very good, but when she was bad she had no equal ". It is also very important to note that most of these girls, during their childhood, had very few friends, and that those friends were never selected on account of age, good work in school or other qualities, but on account of the fact that they were the " bossy " kind, the kind that usually rule and are gang leaders.

In studying the home life of this first group we saw that the parents, though living in America for years, still clung to their old way of looking at things. They were strict, and the children had very little liberty. Athletics, which is a thing practically unknown in European schools, were never encouraged, and as far as the home life was concerned the child was brought up in an atmosphere foreign to America. There is no doubt that a conflict soon started between the old and the new concept. The foreign parents were entirely unable to conceive the nature of American freedom. They lived mostly in crowded sections of the city where the same old ideals prevailed as in their own country. They gathered together, keeping up not only the customs of their own country, but even the language, and for them America was an enigma into which they never penetrated. The children, on the other hand, frequenting our schools and living an American life outside of their homes, were, when back in their homes, under the influence of their parents, with their prejudices and superstitions. The effects were seen when the girl, reaching maturity, went forth into the world to earn her living. It is then that their suggestibility, their credulity, their tractability, played havoc with their personalities. A complete adjustment had never taken place, and as a matter of fact their home life did not prepare such girls for an adjustment. They represented the negative side in the social evolution, and fell easy prey to dark characters and misfortune.

There is another very important point to discuss

here, the absence of religious concepts, the neglect of the spiritual life of these girls. This holds especially true of a certain race where the orthodoxy of the parents found its counterpart in the fact that the children were entirely irreligious. No attempt was made, at all, to give these children anything in the place of the religious concept of the parents. The children were brought up with practically no knowledge of a Deity, except what they got during their school life. The tendency, it seems, was to show their Americanism by irreligiousness—of course, misunderstood Americanism—a faulty conception of liberty and freedom. However, a number of these girls had a religious training in the special schools that they attended, but an inadequate impression was made upon them regarding the ethical aspects of Life's problems.

In studying the case histories, one fact appeared poignant, that is, that up to a certain time these girls were of relatively good character. Then something had always happened, and from that time on the entire life took a different course. In inquiring into these motives, we found that quarrels at home were the starting-point, and then the deplorable acquaintances. There were always persons to give shelter to these girls, but shelter not for their protection, but for their corruption. The law, in this respect, is entirely lax.

One myth should be destroyed in studying the cases, and that is that economic conditions were responsible for their delinquency. Most of these girls had comfortable homes, had opportunities in life and came of respectable families. Some of them had parents in very good circumstances. The life they chose was combined with hardship and want. Not only that, but the girls who became prostitutes rarely made sufficient money to support themselves, and they gave the money they earned to the men with whom they were living. The theory, therefore, that want and poverty are the cause of prostitution does not hold good, at least not in the series which I studied. It appears that the delinquency of these girls, irrespective of the nature of the delinquency, was caused primarily by emotional instability, which was a true emotional defectiveness.

(2) This group represented an evolutionary backstroke, morally. They were entirely unable to adapt themselves to society. They were really not immoral, but amoral. They showed a complete absence of the potentiality of adjustment.

Heredity played an important rôle. In the first place we found a disorganized family life. Alcohol was one of the chief causes. In some cases we found alcoholism in both parents. We found that some of the parents had a notoriously bad name in the neighbourhood, while one mother had a police record. In one family we found more than one member with a bad reputation, and in another one sister was a prostitute, and a brother served a jail sentence. The home atmosphere was very far from healthy—in fact, it was a life of struggle, hardship, quarrels and immorality. Supervision was lax, parents neglected their children, and the child practically brought itself up and led a life without any parental supervision. Here, also, religion played no rôle ; there was neither encouragement nor discouragement in the child's life. All the child's inherited instincts, especially egotism, which should have been moulded in family life, were left to take their own course. The result was that it grew up hyper-egotistic and selfish, and developed without any restraint. We notice that the child-life of these girls was somewhat different. They were troublesome children and later, in school, they were always in trouble with the teachers. They played truant, because they disliked school; they were lazy and could not get along with the other children. Their lives out of school were led by themselves, where they fell prey to the neighbourhood gangsters, and their life of immorality was started before they left school.

Another characteristic of these girls was the ease with which they lied, the ease with which they acquired all that was bad, the ease with which they became adjusted to the criminal surroundings. Among these girls we met the accessory of the gangster in committing a crime; we also met the professional prostitute, with a "steady" to whom she turned over her earnings, and when arrested she refused to accuse him or help the authorities. They showed a great disrespect for their parents, hated them and accused them. Among these girls we saw gang life; we occasionally heard about the use of a gun and we heard them talk about drink and drunken parties. However, the individual girl in this class, though not distinctly feeble-minded, approximated closely to feeble-mindedness in many respects. They did not attain the average mentality, nor the lower end of the average group; they were morons.

The school record showed this too. In spite of the tendency of the teachers to help and push a child ahead in school, it was impossible to do so with them. These children were left behind and never finished the public school course. They left school to go to work.

The after school life is also characteristic. They rarely held a position for any length of time. During a period of one year I counted eight different positions for one girl. The longest time a girl worked at one place was six weeks, and the girl who had eight positions worked altogether only seven months during the 2½ years that she went to work. There was also a great variety in the nature of the work. Some started as telephone operators and finished as factory hands, and in between these occupations they were child's nurse, doctor's office assistant, waitress, finisher in a dressmaker's shop and salesgirl.

It is also to be noticed that the conflict, here, between parents and child was of the greatest. The parents were foreign born and of the type which never assimilated the American life. They were all of the low grade of European peasant or farm labourer. They were like what we call in this country " the white trash ". In this country their occupations were of the same type. Ignorance at home, absence of restraint, moral and otherwise, and a low mentality were sufficient to direct the destinies of these girls in well-defined channels.

If we study the motives which led these girls to delinquency we also find a great difference from the first group. Delinquency had started before the girl left home, and the final break came unexpectedly and impulsively.

But even in this group we fail to find economic conditions as a cause of delinquency. None of these girls became prostitutes or committed larceny for the purpose of bettering their economical state. None of them did it because they were out of work. On the contrary, those committing larceny (shop-lifting, mostly) were working at that time, and those who became prostitutes had no financial benefit thereby. They did it because someone told them to do it, and someone else brought the men to them. Their great emotional instability, their great suggestibility, made them tools in the hands of others, and they would have committed

L

murder just as easily, if they happened to have been told to do so.

It was very interesting to observe the emotionality of these girls. It was just as easy to make them cry as it was to make them laugh. When spoken to about their predicament and the possible outcome of their case, they would show some sorrow, and would ask about the possibility of being set free, and then, a few seconds later, they would show no concern whatever about it. I found that it was possible to awaken some remorse concerning their actions. It was possible to make them feel sorry about their parents, but, as a whole, they did not show very great emotion over it. It was only the thing directly concerned with themselves that was able to evoke in them sorrow, anger, pity or happiness. They were very much concerned about themselves, sometimes displaying a great deal of arrogance, and at other times docility. They were all very anxious to make a good impression upon the examiner, and showed that they were greatly flattered when some attention was paid to them.

A further analysis of the delinquents brought to light a factor which linked them together. We found that their delinquency was the result of an impulsive act which rarely possessed any cognitive elements. Their actions were due to emotional outbursts, usually passing into passions. If, as measured by the mental test, they showed a definite mental retardation, they also showed, emotionally, an approach to the primitive ; a definite emotional defectiveness emerged.

Moreover, a study of the cases, and the conclusions drawn from similar states of emotional instability and defectiveness by other authors, led me to believe that there is a definite organic basis responsible for the condition. This is an organic inferiority expressed in the hereditary endocrine imbalance. Upon such deductions I base my conception of constitutional inferiority, a condition in terms of which the greatest number of delinquents should be classified.

DATE DUE	RETURNED